Words that
Burn Within Me

Hilda Stern Cohen

Words that Burn Within Me

Faith, Values, Survival

DRYAD PRESS  WASHINGTON, D.C.

Consultants: Rosemary Warschawski and Deborah Cohen Katz

The first two hundred copies of this edition are numbered by hand and signed by Werner V. Cohen.

This book is a compilation of prose and poetry written in English or German by Hilda Stern Cohen as selected and arranged by the editors. Portions of this book, *printed in italics*, are based on transcripts of a series of interviews done between May and August 1996 with Hilda Stern Cohen by Gail Rosen. Used by permission.

Hilda Stern Cohen's complete works were first published in Germany under the title *Genagelt ist meine Zunge: Gedichte und Prosa einer Ho-locaust-Überlebenden*. Frankfurt/Main: Bergauf-Verlag, 2003 (ISBN: 3-00-010499-2), edited by Erwin Leibfried and Sascha Feuchert, Research Center for Holocaust Literature, Institute for Modern German Literature, Justus-Liebig University, Giessen, Germany and William Gilcher, Goethe-Institut Washington, DC, in cooperation with Werner V. Cohen.

Hilda Stern Cohen's original notebooks are in the physical custody of Yad Vashem, the Holocaust Martyrs' and Heroes' Authority in Jerusalem.

Rights and acknowledgements continue on page 128.

Publication of this book has been made possible in part thanks to financial support from the Goethe-Institut Washington.

Dryad Press
P.O. Box 11233
Takoma Park, Maryland 20913
www.dryadpress.com; publisher@dryadpress.com

More information at:
www.hildasterncohen.org
www.HildaStory.org

Library of Congress Cataloging-in-Publication Data

Cohen, Hilda Stern, 1924-1997.
  Words that burn within me : faith, values, survival / Hilda Stern Cohen ; edited by Werner V. Cohen, Gail Rosen, and William Gilcher ; translations from the original German by Elborg Forster.
    p. cm.
  ISBN 978-1-928755-10-4 (alk. paper)
  1. Cohen, Hilda Stern, 1924-1997. 2. Jews--Germany--Mücke--Biography.
  3. Holocaust, Jewish (1939-1945)--Poland--Personal narratives. 4. Nieder Ohmen
  (Mücke, Germany)--Biography. I. Cohen, Werner V. II. Rosen, Gail, 1951- III.
  Gilcher, William Harry, IV. Forster, Elborg, 1931- V. Title.
  DS134.42.C64A3 2008
  940.53'18092--dc22
  [B]
                              2008023942

Edited by:
Werner V. Cohen, Gail Rosen, and William Gilcher

Translations from the original German
by Elborg Forster

Table of Contents

Poems by Hilda Stern Cohen
translated by Elborg Forster

Introduction
by Werner V. Cohen

There is a human need to pray, a yearning for connection, an urge to ask for healing, for comfort, for peace. After the Holocaust many said that there is now proof that prayer is futile.

Then there were those, like Hilda, who survived loss and terror, pain and suffering beyond imagining, who were still able to pray and to hold onto faith and trust in God and in God's love for us.

After Hilda's passing I found seven notebooks in the back of a drawer, along with a variety of thoughts put down in writing later in her life. The existence of these notebooks had never been discussed in our fifty years to-gether, and finding them came as a total surprise.

In these notebooks were a large number of penciled poems and prose pieces, all in German and all of very high literary quality.

Dates indicated the year 1946, the year after Hilda's liberation when she was in a Displaced Persons Camp in Austria. There she took the opportunity to gave voice to the stirrings of her soul.

The situations described and the deep insights conveyed gave evidence that she had been a victim of the Nazis and a neutral observer, all at the same time.

She spoke of what it means to preserve one's moral values in a world of utter brutality and degradation. I felt strongly drawn into this darkness and the need to capture it all.

In her writings Hilda does not address the philosophy of Judaism, but each poem and essay is set in the context of values that she herself lived every day. Hilda knew the treasures contained in Judaism. She took it upon herself to perform the spiritual "work" of our family. We observed *kashrut*, the dietary laws, and did this under circumstances that were often difficult. We lived in places where there was no Jewish community. Hilda drew us into strict Sabbath observance. She raised and educated three daughters within the structure of holidays and of the rules of modesty that set them apart from their peers.

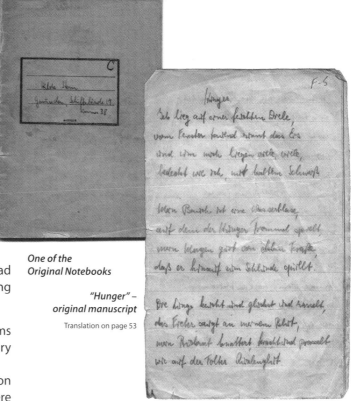

One of the
Original Notebooks

"Hunger" –
original manuscript

Translation on page 53

She was that rare person who lived her own agenda but did not "promote" it. People who interacted with her felt enriched, validated.

On reading her writings, one is aware of a strength of the spirit. She showed decency in actions that were totally counter-instinctual. Thus, she gave food to others who were starving when she herself was lacking in food. She fought for her own survival but never at the expense of others.

She describes the desperation and despair of Jews turning against fellow Jews because of the Nazi "beast" outside the ghetto. She does not judge. She admires the heroism of those who refused to be cruel. She said, "In the end, I have to be grateful, grateful really, that I was never in a position to do anyone harm." She suggests, "You can look into the abyss that is within yourself. This humanity that we all share is for us to deal with, and then transform it into something that's noble."

I share this fond hope.

To Bear Witness

Libraries of books, documentary and literary, have been written on the subject of the Holocaust. Academic careers have been built on it. Visual and tonal artists have been inspired by it. It has been researched and mined by social and political scientists, and the terms of genocide and Nazi have been used sometimes appropriately, and often blasphemously for deep political purposes. The ranks of us who were actual, physical witnesses are rapidly thinning. I have always felt that I could never refuse when asked to tell the story. I have felt that to bear witness is a debt of honor owed to those who could not speak themselves, to my parents and grandparents, the many other family members, and the young man who accompanied us to the ghetto and death. I owe it to those who died for no other reason than being born a Jew.

Now in the evening of my life, which was given me as a gift for which I am humbly grateful, I also want to face away from the past. I want to face my friends and the future. I want to leave you with my witness, but also with a legacy and a challenge. My legacy to you is to incorporate this history into your consciousness and to give the lie to those who would revise and slander any part of it.

My hope and prayer is for peace, security, and dignity, and a full stomach for the children of man. May the darkness of hate and divisiveness yield to the light of a new day!

בע״ה

Hilda Cohen

פייגה בת צבי שאול

(from a presentation written in 1984)

Prayer

Dear God! Now I must pray!
My soul can only stammer in its pain,
The words my lips can stammer are confused.
Oh let me be a child again, let me believe
And talk to You in simple, trusting words.

As I was brought to fathomless abysses
You carried me upon your back as on a path.
A thousand voices of destruction called me,
But deaf and blind to them I walked in safety.

Too hardened is my mouth to thank or beg,
And yet a raging fever burns my soul.
Perhaps I have again strayed far from You –
God, guide me on my way.

Gebet

Mein Gott! Jetzt muß ich beten!
Es stammelt meine Seele ihre Pein,
Es stammeln meine Lippen wirre Worte,
laß mich ein Kind und wieder gläubig sein
und einfach und vertrauend zu Dir reden.

Mein Weg ging über bodenlose Tiefen
auf Deinem Rücken wie auf einem Steg.
Wenn der Vernichtung tausend Stimmen riefen,
ging taub und blind ich sicher meinen Weg.

Steif ist mein Mund zu danken und zu bitten,
doch meine Seele glüht in Fieberpein.
Ich weiß nicht, bin ich wiederum entglitten.
Oh, möchtest weiter Du mein Führer sein.

Time Line

A more detailed chronology is found at the end of the book

January 1, 1924	Hilda is born in the village of Nieder-Ohmen, Germany.
October 1941	Detained by the Gestapo, Hilda and her family are deported to the "Litzmannstadt" ghetto in Lodz, Poland.
March 1944	Hilda's mother and father die of starvation in Lodz.
August 1944	Hilda is transported to Auschwitz-Birkenau, where she is reunited with her sister Carol.
Early 1945	Death March from Auschwitz back to Germany
May 3, 1945	Liberation from Malchow, near Berlin
June 1945	The sisters travel to the Carpathian mountains of Slovakia.
Early Fall 1945	Arrival at an Austrian "Displaced Persons Camp"
July 1946	The sisters leave Europe by ship for the USA.
September 5, 1948	Hilda is married in Baltimore, Maryland.
1952-1956	Birth of three daughters
August 5, 1997	Hilda dies in Baltimore, Maryland.

Source of Texts

This book is based on Hilda Stern Cohen's notebooks and other writings, either translated from the original German or written originally in English. *Those portions of this book printed in italics are based on a series of interviews with Hilda Stern Cohen by Gail Rosen completed between May and August 1996.* The editors have arranged all these texts to create a single overall presentation.

The World of Our Youth

Memories of Chanukah

Come Chanukah in our picture postcard village, and the land lay still under a covering of snow which also covered our home. There were no neon signs or even street lights. My father lit his ancient tin menorah, a candelabra, on the windowsill. It was a family heirloom. We used candles. Oil was used for mother's Chanukah lamp hung from the ceiling. The light of the menorah spreading a circle of coziness and warmth out of our window and down the quiet street inspired me as an eight-year-old to write my first poem. Our treats were walnuts, which we cracked during the half-hour allotted to the burning candles. The usual songs were sung, and our mother's delicious *sufganiot*, doughnuts, sprinkled with confectioner's sugar were served.

I insisted on using a large piece of kindling wood as my own menorah. We played games but did not spin the Dreidel. We played a game known as "Aggravation," *Mensch ärgere dich nicht!*, as well as another homemade board game, for which we used buttons from our mother's button box.

At age ten I decided to write a Chanukah play. A young man a few years older than me directed it. Somebody was Matisyahu, the patriarch of the Chanukah story; others took the part of the Maccabees. I assigned all the roles and enjoyed that very much. The play took place in the Schul, *the synagogue.*

These were among the idyllic moments before the final darkness fell.

I was nine years old when Hitler and the Nazis (*yemach shemam*, May their names be erased!) came to power and eleven when I had to leave the village. No more candles pierced the darkness. I had to experience all twelve years of the Thousand-Year Reich. The final curtain fell on German Jewry (*yee ko me da mam*, God will avenge their blood!).

Four Generations in Nieder-Ohmen, ca. 1935
Front row, left to right: Sister (Carol/Karola), Grandmother (Sara Roth, née Kappenberg), Great-Grandmother (Fanny Kappenberg) with Erna's daughter, Sonja, Grandfather (Jakob Roth) Standing behind: Mother (Hedwig Stern, née Roth), Aunt Erna, Hilda/Hilde

My village is called Nieder-Ohmen. It is located about ninety kilometers northeast of Frankfurt. A few years ago, in 1982, it celebrated its 1,200th anniversary. I don't know how long Jews have lived there, but I think they came with the Romans. Until the end of the eighteenth century, they were the semi-serfs of local feudal lords. Lacking the right of permanent residency, they were forced to move from one village to another. Then they were given permission to settle permanently. Our house had a wooden beam across the main door that revealed that it had been built in 1558. My great-grandfather had purchased the house. He was the first one to be buried in the new Jewish cemetery. There was an older Jewish cemetery in the village which had served many generations.

The German songs of my childhood set up a vibration inside of me, a dissonance of emotion and pain, a reaction so bittersweet. They are the songs I heard around me when growing up, the songs our father loved and made us sing along with him. Often we were hiking over his fields which were spread outside the boundaries of our village, neatly cultivated, carefully marked parcels of land between groupings of trees, little woods free of underbrush, small streams, pleasant green hills.

We sang as we marched through those woods, our feet softly sinking into the decaying mulch beneath, the sun slanting through the trees. On the *Shabbos* afternoons we spent following our father as he was surveying his domain, the feeling of ownership and belonging was palpable in the air.

When I hear the same songs now, all these many years later, I detect shrill and false tones. The air is permeated with the stench of decay, which arises like a fog. The memory of those softly decaying leaves, those hills, and those neat parcels of land is drenched in blood.

The very language of country romance with its flourish towards German womanhood and hunter's horn has an undertone of heavy marching boots. I cannot separate the memory of Dr. Mengele, camp doctor, who represented evil incarnate on the selection platform in Auschwitz, from the German heritage that once was mine.

Our synagogue was an ordinary home that had been remodeled. It had a gallery for women upstairs, just one row deep. There were wooden benches with backs and a slanted board in front to put one's book on, no cushions. We weren't spoiled, though my grandmother had a cushion that she left there. The place was always full. I went with my grandmother and my mother. We had the strict decorum of an Orthodox synagogue, but kids were running around upstairs and downstairs.

Religious education in Germany was not strictly separated from secular subjects. As a consequence the local pastor was allowed to come into the public school to give religious instruction. Our own Jewish teacher was also allowed to come in and give instruction. We learned the Aleph-Bet and a few basic prayers. There weren't enough Jewish children to divide into classes. We all learned to read and were able to follow prayers in synagogue.

Sabbath was the time to get together. After attending synagogue in the morning, we would go on an extended walk in the afternoon, children behind and parents in front. It was called a Spaziergang, *a promenade. Our Christian neighbors did it on Sundays, and we did it on Sabbath. We would always take the same route and end up in the next village. That never changed.*

Growing up as a Jewish child in rural Germany before Hitler came to power was a balancing act into which we were born and which we took for granted.

The village where my sister and I, as well as both parents, grandparents, and numerous relatives were born and raised had a Christian population of about fourteen hundred people, all Lutheran. Buildings connected to worship were the ancient church, dating back to the Reformation, and our inconspicuous synagogue. The Jewish community, dating back to the late middle ages, had never numbered more than thirty families.

Our family seemed to be well integrated into the village population, speaking the local peasant dialect with our neighbors and trading village gossip and confidences over the back fence. Our parents (*z"l, zichronam livracha,* May their memory be for a blessing!) spoke high German in the home and did not look favorably on my sister and myself using the local dialect even with our schoolmates. My mother (*z"l*) never failed to mutter *l'havdil,* to make a distinction, whenever she mentioned us in connection with the Gentile children, our school, and playmates.

Our parents' social life was almost exclusively within the small Jewish community in which two family names predominated: that of Stern (my maiden name) and Roth (my mother's maiden name). While there was a distinct chance of marriage between relatives, this was mostly avoided by means of an annual Purim ball in the springtime during which young people from other villages, whose names were often also Roth or Stern, were introduced to each other for the purpose of matrimony.

Another building of importance in our Jewish life was the *mikveh,* the ritual bath. It was overseen by a Gentile woman who was notified, usually by the children of the house, to ready the premises and heat the bathwater. Telephones were not in all homes in those days.

Religious instruction for us children was dispensed on a released class time basis by our teacher, who served as a *kli kodesh,* an all-purpose functionary, . He was hired by the congregation, the *Kehillah,* through the good offices of the *Landesrabbiner,* the district rabbi. His was a demanding and often thankless job for little pay. These teachers were the forgotten heroes of Jewish life in rural Germany and constituted a lifeline for countless generations. While assimilation of Jewish life went on apace in the cities, it was much slower, often nonexistent, in the countryside where Jews had lived in the same unchanged way for hundreds of years.

My father (*z"l*), like many Jews in rural Germany, was a cattle dealer. This occupation was necessitated by the repressive laws of the past that forbade Jews to own land but allowed them to trade cattle, a service useful to the local farmers. During our grandfather's lifetime, he was able to buy some land. Our father had increased his holdings. We were, however, the only Jewish family with a little farm.

Our neighbors were well aware of our holidays and often served as *Shabbos goyim,* performing necessary tasks for us on the Sabbath. There was no display of distinctive clothing, beards, *tzitzis,* or *taleisim* worn publicly. Even *kipot* were not worn, but hats, which were a common head-covering for Jews and non-Jews alike. Certainly, *Shabbos* finery was worn. To sum up, great care was taken not to affront the dominating conformity and homogeneity of German society. Talk about a balancing act!

Karola/Carol and Hilde/Hilda, ca. 1928

My early childhood was quite idyllic. Our village was surrounded by the fields. We had a wagon pulled by cows. Wealthier farmers had horses, a distinct status symbol. For my father, it didn't pay to maintain horses. I enjoyed sitting on the wagon with a board laid across it. We would drive out there and would help to turn the hay. My sister and I were little, so we would play around in the fields. We took lunch to our people who worked out in the fields. We enjoyed ourselves.

We had an extended family. My maternal grandparents lived within walking distance. My paternal grandfather lived with us in the house, as did my father's unmarried brother and sister. My mother had married my father at the age of twenty. She had her hands full. There was a pump in the house. We had no running water.

When my sister Carol, Karola, was three years old, she liked to try new foods. Our neighbors had a trough to feed their ducks. They fed them stinging nettles, which grew wild by the roadsides, mixed with potatoes. Touching these plants would cause blisters all over. I saw my sister eating out of that trough, and I said to my mother, "Look what she's eating." Carol said, "It's very good. It's very good." She had no ill effects from sharing with the ducks.

We played games. My sister had lots of ideas. If one doesn't have fancy toys, one uses everything possible for toys, very inventively. With us, no box ever went to waste.

My sister would crawl in a box, and we would have long conversations. "I'm Mrs. This and you're Mr. That." We created whole families! And every morning, particularly on Shabbos, when my parents were up already, we'd crawl on my parents' beds. They had twin beds, and she would make a big tent over her head. We would gossip about all the neighbors. She was good at imitating people with theatrical flair. This could go on for hours.

When Carol was little, she feared leaving my parents, especially my father. On visits to relatives in another village, Carol would develop stomach cramps. In the villages there was no running water. Toilets were outside the house. She would cry there in the dark while I stood in front of her. I assured her that she would be okay and that I would see to it that she would be able to go home. Her pains immediately stopped.

Village Children

Many customs of the village dated back to the Middle Ages. Every afternoon, a man in a uniform, the town crier, came around shaking his bell. Children would run up to find out what was going on. He called out the news of the day then went on throughout the village.

There was a newspaper that was published in Giessen, a neighboring town. It did not deal with our village's news. Anything the mayor wanted the village to know, anything of an official nature, the town crier would announce.

My sister was very popular. All the children liked to play with her because she was very inventive. In my grandmother's back yard there were a lot of beanpoles. Some ten or fifteen of them were heaped together in one corner. They were used to support vines that grew up on them. We always helped mother and my aunt in their gardens and enjoyed it. I was very fond of reading German mythology, such stories as the Nibelungen, the wars of Siegfried and Brunhilde. I would take the position of a queen while my friend, a little boy called Otto, was my king. Then we would throw beanpoles. They were our lances.

We were part of the village, its children, growing up there and being treated by our neighbors very well. I taught myself to read by going around neighbors' houses looking at their canisters, which said "flour," "salt," and such until I figured out what they said. Finally, I decided I could write too. I must have been around five. So I scribbled something, and I asked my mother what I had written. She said, "I don't know. It doesn't make any sense." I then took it across to my neighbor Karl, who was a blacksmith. He worked in a fascinating place where sparks were flying in the dark. I handed it to Karl, and he read it. He made it up, but he read me a whole megillah, a whole story. I went to my mother and said, "I don't know what's the matter with you. Karl can read everything I wrote." We had a close relationship.

There was a wedding of our back-door neighbor. He was the mayor of Nieder-Ohmen. We were extremely close with them. I was always in their house. I have a picture of the wedding. You can see the bride and groom, everyone dressed in black. They didn't want to waste the money for white. It was not practical. Carol and I were dressed up with wreaths on our heads, like flower girls. Carol refused to wear the wreath.

The wedding was in the Lutheran Church. We were allowed to go because we were little. My parents didn't go.

Hilda (front left) and Carol (front right) at Conrad Carle's Wedding, November, 1928

The mayor's mother was quite religious. She used to say, "What they do to the Jews will come back to haunt us." She knew it. She was always careful about food when we ran into her house. She gave us either hard-boiled eggs or fruit to eat, something that she knew was kosher. On Fridays she'd say, "Go home. Your mother wants you home for Shabbos."

It was a very pleasant childhood. We were friendly with everybody until Hitler came to power in 1933, and then everything changed overnight. I was nine years old.

The Lost Knife, a story

The Nazis passed an ordinance that forbade kosher slaughtering in Germany. Some kosher meat was imported from other countries. Most religious Jews could not afford this meat. While it would have been dangerous to slaughter large animals, some *shochtim* (kosher butchers) continued to kill chickens in secret for their friends and families. Herta's grandfather was a *shochet* in the village where she was born. Jewish families there depended on him to supply them with kosher chickens and meat. Her grandfather, Jacob, took this risk and continued to slaughter a few chickens and other fowl for *Shabbos*, just for the family.

On Thursday afternoon, on a wintry day, grandfather Jacob prepared to come to Herta's house to *shecht* (ritually slaughter) a chicken for their *Shabbos* meal.

Since a special knife is required in performing this functional ritual prescribed by law, the grown-ups thought that nine-year-old Herta could be safely entrusted to carry it from the grandparents' house to that of her parents. Perhaps they also thought that a child might not be suspected of carrying anything forbidden. Her grandmother carefully wrapped the long narrow knife in newspapers and sent her on her way home, carrying the little package.

Herta knew that the task was a very important one. She felt that great trust had been placed upon her by her family, and she prayed to *HaShem* (literally "the Name," meaning God) that she would carry it out without fail. She had always been teased about being a bookworm and a dreamer, but this time she would show them.

There was a mixture of fear and pride in her heart as she clutched her parcel, peering around corners, walking sometimes fast and sometimes slow. The distance between her grandfather's and her parents' home was not very great, and she walked it almost daily. All the streets, all the houses, all the farmyards, all the people were familiar to her.

On this day everything seemed changed. The houses seemed grayer and closer together, the mud in the village street seemed to cling more to her sturdy boots, people didn't seem to smile when they answered her greeting. Moreover, the way to her parents' house seemed much longer.

When she finally arrived there, her heart was pounding; perspiration covered her forehead, and her hands that clutched her precious parcel felt clammy.

She ran to her mother and proudly handed it over, thinking that she had accomplished a task not only for her family, but also, somehow for the Jewish people. Her mother unwrapped the newspaper. The knife was gone.

Her heart skipped a beat and then began to race. The fear made it hard for her to breathe. She had been negligent once again. She had not guarded her secret as she had been admonished. She had been the absent-minded dreamer the adults had so often said she was. Had she now endangered the whole *Kehillah*, the whole Jewish community, of her village with her neglect? Would the Nazis find the knife and know that the Jews were not obeying the laws of the Third Reich? Would they find her grandfather, Jacob, and imprison him or worse?

No one said anything to her. They just shook their heads in disgust and disappointment. The day dragged on, and everyone went about their business in worried silence. Herta's mother started to prepare dinner and set the kitchen table. Everything was so quiet. It made her want to scream or throw something. She didn't feel like eating, but she was told to sit down with the family and she did.

It turned dark outside, and there was still homework, to do. She undid her school bag and cleared a place at the kitchen table.

The heavy front door squeaked as it was opened. Grandfather Jacob's deep voice and firm footsteps could be heard. She pushed away her books and ran out to find out the latest news. There was a smile on his face! He grabbed her and lifted her up. "It's all right," he said, "the knife has been found." "By whom, by whom?" she asked, anxiously.

"A Gentile woman, a friend, found it in the street. She knew it belonged to me and returned it."

"Did she know it was the *shechita* knife? Will she tell anyone else?"

"I don't know if she knew what it was for, but don't worry. I think it is going to be fine. *HaShem* has been with us."

Changing Times

My parents considered themselves very much part of the village, but also you might say they knew their place, as did all Jews. Hitler came to power around Pesach (Passover) time in 1933. Immediately, like out of nowhere, it was the Nazi party with brown shirts and all the paraphernalia. They organized what they called a boycott. They stationed themselves in front of all the Jewish homes, telling the non-Jews, "You cannot go to them. Your children can't play with the Jewish kids." They stood there the whole day. Being on one side of the barricade, I looked across to my friends, and they were standing there. We were looking at each other. I don't think they understood any more than we did what was going on.

These were not people from outside the village; they were people my parents went to school with. They knew them very well. Then, they held a phony weapons search. They knew well that nobody in Nieder-Ohmen owned weapons. My father was a First World War veteran, and he had a bayonet, a souvenir from the war. My mother realized that's what he had brought home from the war, and she was scared. She thought they'd find it and arrest him. In Germany at that time, we didn't have any built-in cabinets. We had an armoire. It was a very heavy piece of furniture. My mother brought the bedroom furniture into the marriage as her dowry. She stuck the bayonet behind it so the Nazis wouldn't find it. They came in, and there was a friend of my mother's, a schoolmate, and she said, "Heinrich, you know we don't have any weapons."

"Well," he said, "the Führer said you can't trust the Jews. They are out to annihilate the German people." They searched, but they didn't find it.

This certain man and his family were the staunchest Nazis, and a lot of other people were scared of him. But strangely enough, his daughter was a good friend of my sister's. They played together in school until we couldn't go there anymore. This girl always pointed out the difference between her and my sister, that she was Aryan and German and my sister was not.

I was in the third grade in 1933 and went to school for a couple more years. There was one teacher who had been brought in from outside. He was a Nazi party member who was to teach the other teachers how to be proper National Socialists and what to teach the children. Soon the Jewish children had to sit in front. Children had to stand up when their teacher came in and had to say "Guten Morgen." That changed now, and they had to say, "Heil Hitler." I raised my hand but was told, "Jew, put your hand down." A teacher actually said that. It was shocking because nobody had ever talked like that before. People were being indoctrinated, and they let themselves be indoctrinated. They were open to it. Later they wanted it to be known that they didn't cooperate, but they did.

There was a family down the street from us with a lot of boys who started to pick on us, especially on me. They used to throw stones. My sister would go and talk to them, engage them in small talk, some nonsense. She would signal me from her back to run behind her back so I wouldn't be exposed to stone throwing. It was like a gauntlet, and she always protected me.

My father's comrades who had fought with him in the war knew that my father was a very patriotic German. After the boycott they were scared to come to our house. One man would come as late as ten or eleven o'clock at night, or they would meet secretly. He would always tell my father, "This guy Hitler is no good. He's just a wall painter, a nobody. You and I know the German people are not going to keep him. He is going to be kicked out. You don't have to leave here because he won't last until the next election." But there wasn't another election.

Most of the Jewish people in the village came to the United States. A few went to Palestine and other countries in the world, wherever they could get in, even South America. They heeded the warnings. My aunt got out just at the last minute. Only three or four families got caught.

My father thought it was going to change. So we stayed. Those few good friends thought that they knew better. A fatal mistake.

Boycott, a story

The Nazi Party of Flensungen proclaimed a boycott of Jewish businesses during Passover. The national party had commanded them to do so, and they were anxious to show their compliance.

Their leader called a rally and fired them up with many long words about conniving Bolshevik, Capitalist enemies and parasites sucking the blood of all people, of which the Jews were the worst. Fortified by this speech, they put on their Nazi shirts with swastika armbands and stuck their mandatory guns in their holsters. Marching down the streets of Flensungen in their freshly polished boots, they sang the Party hymn: *"Wenn das Judenblut vom Messer spritzt,…"* ("When Jewish blood spurts from the knife…").

In the center of the village, Heinrich, their leader, gave them orders. There was some confusion since there were few Jewish businesses in Flensungen. Most of the Jews were engaged in cattle trading and agriculture. How was one to boycott a stable? The problem was quickly solved by Heinrich's decision to boycott the Jews' front doors, regardless of whether they had a proper business or not.

Herta Ginsberg's father owned a small farm in addition to his cattle-trading business. There was a large compost heap between the house and the barn. The Party members could not immediately decide where to station themselves, but finally three of them opted for the front door. The house was surrounded by the houses of the Ginsberg family's Gentile neighbors. Herta's non-Jewish friends always came to visit her, or she would visit them. Sometimes they would meet in each other's back yard where they played.

On this day, however, everything seemed changed. The children were there, but they stayed behind the men in the uniforms, peeking out, going back into their houses, and sometimes coming back out. They would shuffle back and forth. One or the other might say something, and they would break into giggles, again running inside, slamming their door. But soon they would come out again.

For a long time, Herta stayed in her living room, peering between the plants and lace curtains to watch the Party members and her friends. At first the uniforms, the swastika, and the guns intimidated her. But after a few hours she became bored; it all seemed like a masquerade. The people wearing those uniforms were familiar to her; they were residents of the village. Some of them had been childhood friends and schoolmates of her parents. And the children out there, they were her friends. She had played with them almost every day of her life except for bad weather or some sore throats in winter. She sat next to them on the long school benches with an inkpot for each child. Often they would come to her to help them with homework because she was good at writing fanciful compositions and she liked school.

Finally she stepped out the front door and stood on the cobblestone walk. The Party men who had been marching back and forth, seemingly not knowing what to do with themselves, suddenly stood still and turned to face her. The children appeared behind them and between their legs.

Herta first kicked the loose cobblestones and ran up and down the walk a few times. Then she also stood still and looked at the children seemingly stuck between the Nazi men. She tried a smile and waved. But they did not wave back. Behind the backs of the Nazi men, they were saying things to each other. The Nazi men turned to the children and laughed. The children laughed too. Then they were silent. Someone threw a stone. It didn't hit Herta, but it hit the heavy house door with a thud.

The door opened, and Herta's mother called her in. "You should know better than to go out at a time like this." Herta ran upstairs and sat on the floor beside her bed where she had left a book half read. It was a romantic novel about German medieval knights and their ladies. She tried to continue reading, but it was difficult at first. With determination, her eyes tried to focus on the familiar Gothic script, and soon she was off with a beautiful maiden in a dark and leafy forest with a view of a sunny clearing bordering a calm and clear lake. Nothing moved but a few bees and butterflies around the sleepy heads of daisies and snapdragons. And yes, there appeared the knight in his cumbersome armor, galloping towards her. He stopped, dismounted. Her heart skipped. He had dark flashing eyes, and there was a Star of David on his shield.

She must have dozed off. There was her mother's voice. "They are gone, dear. Come down for the second *Seder.*"

Nieder-Ohmen.
The Stern family home
on the Hintergasse,
today's Rathausgasse,
as it appeared ca.
1910-1920.
Great-grandfather
Abraham Stern
purchased the house,
built in 1558, in 1871.

(courtesy Heinrich Reichel,
Nieder-Ohmen)

About 1935, when I was in fifth grade, we could no longer go to the school in the village. My parents decided to send me to the Samson Raphael Hirsch School in Frankfurt. I lived there with my aunt and uncle. I had to learn so much in one year because it was a Jewish day school, and the kids had learned an awful lot by the time I got there. In one year I had to catch up to them. I was totally charmed and seduced by that and enjoyed it, though it wasn't easy leaving my parents.

I wasn't happy with my aunt and uncle. My parents were very happy, and my grandparents were ecstatically happy with each other, so I took that for granted. Then I found out that my aunt and uncle did not have a happy marriage. I suddenly realized that grownups have tensions; grownups don't always get along with each other. That was a traumatic experience for me. I did tell my father about it. It was his sister after all, so he did not want to hear about it. My father, it seemed to me, was a "straight shooter," very honest. It was something he emphasized to us over and over again. I thought he was the epitome of virtue. So I was somewhat stunned when I found out that he knew this but apparently didn't want to acknowledge it. I was still a little girl, really.

There was persecution. The noose was tightening around our necks, and I was aware of it. But whatever happens, one continues growing up. I became a teenager, went through puberty and was already very much on my own. My sister, who was a little younger, was sent to a Jewish boarding school in Bad Nauheim, a nearby town. It was a happy experience for her because she was together with a lot of other Jewish kids.

A Safe Place

In 1937, at the end of the year in Frankfurt, I was offered the opportunity to go to the Training Seminary for Jewish Teachers in Würzburg (the *Israelitische Lehrerbildungsanstalt* or ILBA). I attended there for the next year and a half, and that proved to be an island of safety and warmth – not just spiritual, but physical too. A different world opened up to me. The impact that this period of my life had on me, and the rest of my family much later, would be crucial.

At ILBA we became "support groups" for each other. We stimulated each other intellectually and spiritually. We knew that the threats and dangers surrounding us were very real. Our needs for structure and continued education were met, and the vicious onslaught against Jewish pride and identity bounced off a bulwark of faith in *HaShem* and the singularity of His people.

I was privileged to live in this environment. Even then I didn't take it for granted. At school the first day one had to pass an entrance exam. My father took me. He had to wait until the end of the day to find out whether I had been accepted. In the afternoon I had to take exams in subjects I never had before, like formal music. It was a non-Jewish teacher who examined us. He played the notes and wanted me to tell him what he had played, the names of the notes. I guessed the whole thing. Afterwards I went out to my father and said, "It looks like I have passed it."

My father said, "Well, you are very lucky." He was not one to praise a lot. Out of his pocket he took a shiny apple and said, "That's for you." That was the highest praise he could give me. He left me there. I was thirteen.

The school had instituted a special course for children who had come from secular schools. They were given a year of an intensive course so that they could fit into their new Orthodox environment. I was the lowest on the totem pole there because I was

very young, but everyone was encouraging. The close and supportive relationship of the students towards each other made an indelible impression on me. Help in strengthening my Jewish studies was given freely and generously by older students.

The school functioned in the style of a yeshiva. *One studied with partners and had the input of an older student who was one's mentor. There was a girl named Bella Brockman who was seven years older than me. She was doing student teaching to get her certificate. She used me as a guinea pig, waking me up when I should have been sleeping, and giving dramatic presentations that she was preparing for her class. One night the secretary of the school came home late and saw a light on in our room. The next day she let Bella have it because she was depriving me of sleep. We were well taken care of. The teachers were excellent. Often they were Jewish university professors dismissed from universities.*

We had Shabbos *together, and services were held in the school. It gave us the pride that we needed. We became aware that it was good to be a Jew, that it was an honorable, even a special thing to be a Jew. No matter what anybody said on the outside, they were always in the wrong. My father used to quote a German poem, "Your thoughts are free." The realization that there existed inner freedom gave us something to live up to.*

We had lectures on Shabbos, *usually before* Havdalah, *the ceremony to mark the end of* Shabbos. *Our rabbi would speak. He couldn't turn on the lights because it was still* Shabbos. *He would stand there in the long hall with a small night light behind him. It was just wonderful, mystical. There was a real aura in that building. It felt very safe. We felt amongst our own. One didn't have to be constantly on alert. One could let down, let go.*

I was there for a year and a half, until Kristallnacht.

Kristallnacht

On November 7, 1938, Erich vom Rath, Third Counselor at the German Embassy in Paris, had been shot by Hershel Grynspan, a seventeen-year-old Polish Jew whose parents had been deported from Germany a few weeks earlier. The Nazis saw this as their long awaited opportunity to wage war against the Jews.

On November 9, 1938, the day vom Rath died, they precipitated the so-called *Kristallnacht*, a pogrom that was alleged to have been a spontaneous reaction by the German people.

Synagogues and Jewish homes were burned, looted, and destroyed in every city and hamlet in Germany and Austria. Jewish men and teenagers were arrested, and about thirty thousand of them were sent to Concentration Camps.

Just before *Kristallnacht*, laws were passed affecting foreigners of Eastern European parentage. In Germany it was very difficult to become a citizen of the country. Offspring of foreigners, even those born in Germany, were not automatically entitled to citizenship.

At least half of the students at the seminary were of Eastern European parentage. Born in Germany, they spoke without an accent. Also because, in most cases, their parents had been married by a rabbi, they were not considered legally married in Germany. Offspring of these very Orthodox families had to take their mother's names, as if they were illegitimate. This was an embarrassment to them, and it wasn't true at all.

Then one day these foreign students were rounded up and sent to Poland. The Poles did not let them in, and they were stranded in no-man's land. The population of the school had suddenly shrunk to half.

Last Days of the Seminary

At 2 a.m. during the night of November 9, 1938, the janitor came to wake us up. We were the seven or eight female students housed on the upper floor of the building adjacent to the seminary. I was not quite 15 years old at the time and had never been up at such an unusual hour, a fact that made an enormous impression on me. The other girls were moving around the hallway, and several entered my room to tell me to get dressed.

The janitor, a non-Jew, was standing near the window looking out toward the town of Würzburg: "They are burning the synagogues, and I heard that a whole gang is heading this way. Take my advice and get out of the building. They are sure to ransack the seminary and, who knows, perhaps come right up to your rooms." We knew who "they" were and needed no further encouragement.

The road into town was filled with marching stormtroopers and Hitler Youth moving toward the seminary. We started to walk away, out into the peaceful autumnal countryside.

We had been taking sewing lessons at a convent nearby, and the nuns were known to us, if not as friends, then at least as benevolent strangers. Their pious demeanor seemed to indicate that they were beyond the propaganda of the Third Reich, and their allegiance was to their religious faith, something we could understand and with which we could identify. Instinctively, we headed for the convent.

The massive medieval buildings were enclosed by a deep stone wall, and the gate, which was usually open, was shut. We realized that the early morning hours were not the best time to get the attention of sleeping nuns. Soon, however, we noticed that quite a few of them were engaged in an early morning prayer procession, walking silently in single file around the buildings, carrying candles, their dark habits billowing.

We banged at the gate and called out to them over and over again, but they did not seem to hear us. The iron gate remained closed. I felt personally outraged and betrayed, because I had trusted in their aura of devotion and impartial kindness.

As the dawn lightened the sky, we became aware of tire-tinted smoke rising from the city. Synagogues and Jewish homes and businesses were burning. We could not stay near the convent walls in indecision, so we headed toward Würzburg. The streets were deserted and still dark, our footsteps the only sound around us.

Soon, however, we had a companion. A man on a motorcycle, wearing a leather outfit and goggles, followed us silently and slowly. We tried to dodge him by changing over to the other side of the street or quickly entering side alleys. He kept stubbornly at our heels, a silent, ghostly personification of evil forces let loose that night.

We finally arrived at the home of the synagogue president. Inside the apartment people were moving back and forth, coming in with the latest reports from the streets, being given refreshments, and leaving again. During the hours I spent in that home, I was never able to figure out who belonged to the family, and who, like myself, was there for temporary shelter. It was much, I would imagine, like military headquarters of a besieged city.

I decided to call my parents, who were still living in Nieder-Ohmen. I was able to talk to my mother and found her distraught and near panic. Our home had been ransacked, and my father had been arrested and sent to the Buchenwald Concentration Camp. My mother was alone in Nieder-Ohmen. We agreed that we would meet in Frankfurt. My sister was safe in her school in Bad Nauheim, for the time being.

It was not possible to retrieve any of my belongings from the seminary. Someone must have lent me money because I went to the train station and bought a ticket for Frankfurt.

On the train I tried to make myself as inconspicuous as possible, not too difficult for a 100-pound, five-foot-two-inch girl. The compartment in which I traveled was occupied by Nazi Party members, some in uniform, in addition to housewives and rank-and-file male citizens. There was much discussion about the "political events" and the "deserved punishment" of the "Jewish swine" for the murder of a German attaché in Paris. I felt very conspicuous, cowering in my corner of the compartment.

I was afraid to use public transportation in Frankfurt. I walked to the home of my biology teacher from the Samson Raphael Hirsch School. Dr. Fuchs was a stocky, red-haired lady much concerned with her students' hygiene and general health habits. I headed for her apartment and strangely again a motorcyclist accompanied me wordlessly and would not leave my side. I shuddered.

I arrived in exhaustion, and as I came up the stairs Dr. Fuchs ushered me into her comfortable apartment and looked at me questioningly. She gave me warm milk and said, "We will discuss everything tomorrow." She gave me supper and prepared a bed. As she dimmed the light, she handed me a copy of Christian Morgenstern's poems. I went to sleep reading poetry.

I vaguely remember going back to Würzburg some weeks later to pick up some of my belongings. The place was quite empty. There was an air of finality, a distinct message that a chapter in the history of the German Jews had come to an end.

My father was released from Buchenwald Concentration Camp after several weeks. He was freed supposedly because he was a Frontsoldat, *a frontline soldier in the First World War. My father was then drafted to a road gang in Silesia. He was quite proud that he was in such good physical shape that he could swing the heavy hammer. He talked about that and how much it meant to him.*

Hedwig Roth Stern *Meier Stern*

Waiting in Suspense

My parents remained in Nieder-Ohmen. Of all the Jews, they were the last ones there. After Kristallnacht, they had to sell their property. The people who bought our house did have to pay a sum of money, but the Reich collected it all. My parents were allowed to live in one room upstairs, and they worked on the farm for the new owners in exchange for food. They stayed there for another year and then moved to Frankfurt.

Shopping hours for Jews had been drastically restricted, and we could only shop at certain stores. We could not enter entertainment establishments such as the opera, theaters, movies, or any public function. Even public parks were restricted to us.

These laws were easy to enforce since at about that time we received through the mail for each individual two Stars of David to be sewn on our outerwear, one in front and one in back. Dire punishment was threatened for any Jew, child or adult, caught without a star.

At the age of fifteen, I, together with many other Jewish girls and women, was drafted to work in German industry. Since we were still in Frankfurt and the work was fairly clean, in a large book bindery, I didn't think of it as a great hardship, even though we had to walk back and forth to work, not being allowed to use public transportation.

Jewish men and Jewish women had to adopt the additional names of Israel and Sarah, respectively. These symbols and names, the Star of David and the Hebrew names, were meant to degrade us in the eyes of our non-Jewish neighbors and, perhaps, in our own eyes. I don't know if they succeeded with the population, most of whom, I am afraid, had already become conditioned, if they ever needed it, to see us through Nazi eyes. As for ourselves, certainly for myself, these symbols and names constituted the pride and honor of the Jewish people, and I am proud that the Star of David has become the national symbol of the State of Israel, as it may have been in the time of King David.

My sister, who is fourteen months younger than me, and was fourteen years old then, was transported with about two hundred other Jewish girls from Frankfurt to Berlin to work in a munitions factory owned and run by Siemens-Schuckert (Siemens is still a German industrial giant). The girls, and many others, were used as forced labor and kept under guard, deprived of freedom of movement.

I will not waste time now telling about our mood at a time when the war had started. Initial bombing attacks from England took place while we cowered in cellars with our enemies, who sometimes refused us entry, always being verbally and frequently physically abused. In our hearts we cheered the Allied attacks, hoping against hope that the war would come to an end soon, while at the same time the doors for escape were closing with finality, and the German *Blitzkrieg* began to overtake all of Europe.

We still got a few postcards from my sister while we were in Frankfurt, but she had really disappeared from our lives. My parents never saw her again.

It was like an in-between time, the time when the war started on September 1, 1939, and the time when we were deported – a two-year interval. It was as though we were living on the "Isle of the Damned."

I was coming into puberty. Things were going on inside of me, which to some extent overshadowed what went on outside. I was very conscious of myself, more than I wanted to be while being confronted with what went on outside myself. I found it very exciting to grow up, to become a woman.

My school in Würzburg had closed. I went to my sister's school in Bad Nauheim. After three months that closed too. I went to Frankfurt, where a cousin of my father was the director of the Philanthropin, a secular Jewish school – very good academically, but not religious at all. I spent another few months there until it was closed too. My grandparents also had to leave the village, and our whole family was suddenly brought closer in a way that they had not planned.

In Frankfurt, I had exposure to things I had never experienced and met people I would never have met. I was very intrigued with a lady, a Mrs. Grier who came from an elite Jewish family. As a young lady, she was employed in the Kaiser's household. She worked with the children. I guess she was a maid, really. There were chamber pots with the crest of the German Kaiser on the bottom in gold. Her fortune, which had apparently been extensive, had shrunk to a point where she now lived in an apartment near us. She had just a few rooms, and she had the remnants of her glory all around her – cute figurines and beautiful collectibles.

Mrs. Grier wrote poetry. She was taller than average with a slim figure. She dressed well, though somewhat unusually, in flowing clothes. She had long gray hair that she wore in a bun, and she often wore a very large hat. She played the piano, and her daughter, who was a little older than I, maybe nineteen, played the violin. They had these little musical evenings. She'd invite people like me, a fifteen-year-old, because she had no other audience left.

A German soldier, who was still faithful to the family, used to come to visit. I had acquired a boyfriend, and I schlepped him there too. We both sat there totally entranced. She was so ladylike and to me everything beautiful that one could imagine, really from another world.

We were drafted at the same time, had to work at the same factory, and she also had to wear the Yellow Star. She was a Jew, though I don't think one could call her Jewish in the sense in which I think of being Jewish. She and her husband were not connected with any synagogue or any kind of Jewish lifestyle. They both were Jews by birth.

Her husband had gone to England with her son. She told me about a lifestyle that was totally foreign to me. She had affairs, and he had affairs, and they were living happily with each other. I don't know if she had any religion whatsoever, and if she did, it was very eclectic.

We lived in a kind of no-man's land. Everybody tried in frantic ways to prepare for emigration. I was enrolled in a class learning to be a waitress, where the teacher was a waiter from Vienna who liked young girls. He'd come awfully close to us sometimes. But the whole thing was kind of funny.

We had pity for each other. He was a dirty old man, it's true, but he was a sad man, and so was everybody else. The adults seemed to have become trapped. They seemed so helpless. One does not like to see adults of one's parents' age be so helpless. The young ones among us, young ones under eighteen, seemed more vital, healthier, more competent.

There was a strange role reversal that took place psychologically, as it did also later in the camps. Adults who had lived a life from which they had gained certain expectations were suddenly confronted with an abyss. There were no signs, no gateposts, none of the usual milestones that one could follow. Everything had fallen away. Children, young children, who have no real expectations, to whom everything is exciting and totally new anyway, could cope better. We were in uncharted waters where nobody had been before. So we had pity for these older people. Since there were no more guideposts, there was nobody to say to us, "This you don't do. You do that."

I made friends with a young girl my age who took me to a friend's house. The friend was dancing, slow dancing in the apartment to a tango, with a young man who was her half-brother. I found out that they had a relationship, and she got pregnant. These were things that I saw, that I could not tell my parents and that I had to puzzle about and try to make sense of.

I became friends with another young woman who was also considerably older than I. I found out that she had an illegitimate child. It was very painful for me. I almost fainted because I had such love, such faith in her. I told my father about that. I told him what her reasons were. I don't remember the reasons anymore. My father said to me, "Everyone is his own best advocate." That's all he said. He did not forbid me to see her anymore. I went to see the child. The child was in a home and later was killed. I don't know what happened to my friend. She just disappeared.

People ask me, "What did your parents do during that time?" I don't remember. I think it was an empty time. Various edicts came. We could only buy food in certain grocery stores. We could only sit in the park on certain benches and during certain times. Jews could only inhabit so many square meters. We lived all in one apartment together. There were no more movies, cinemas. Then we were drafted into this factory, the bookbindery. When we had to go to work, we had to walk there, because we could not use streetcars. We were used to walking, and we walked together. Mrs. Grier and I had the most interesting conversations.

It was a factory setting, and it was very different from the life I had known. They made propaganda material for the army. It was piecework, putting together little pamphlets. It was clean and not backbreaking work, and because we worked we got extra coupons for food. We went into a freight elevator. There a foreman showed us all kinds of obscene pictures. It was a totally different world, but we were together.

In the factory one of the managers or one of the owners came past. Mrs. Grier said, "I know him very well. We used to be in the same social group." He went past her and past her, back and forth and back and forth. Obviously he was struggling to do something. All of a sudden, he stopped and said, "Mrs. Grier, what are you doing here?" That was a typical question when they did not know what else to say. He knew she was a Jew. She answered something very dignified. I was very proud of her. He just shook his head and went on.

All productive work was measured and recorded. Everything was so well documented in Germany. It stood me in good stead after the war because they actually found my Arbeitsbuch, my labor certificate, which proved that I worked for the German State. It was stamped with a big J (for Jew). I did not have any kind of documentation whatsoever. It took me about six months to remember the name of the firm I had worked for. Then all of a sudden, all came back to me. I wrote to my lawyer, and they went through the files, and they found me. On the basis of that, I receive social security payments from Germany, not just restitution but social security for having been a slave worker. It's weird, but I get paid a few dollars now for the work I did then.

By that time I was putting my toes in the water outside the Orthodox community and wanted to find out what everybody was all about. In Frankfurt there was a Zionist organization, Shomer Hazair, a Socialist group. I decided since I was floating around that I was going to volunteer for Shomer Hazair. That was where I met Horst Appel.

Horst had been in a preparatory program for people who wanted to emigrate to Palestine. It was called Hachshara. They sent kids from the city to farms to show them how to work on the land. Some of them had come to us in Nieder-Ohmen, and we had to show them how to make hay and plant things, something *that was an everyday occurrence to us. We thought it was rather amusing. Horst had been in* Hachshara *in eastern Germany, and he came away with tuberculosis. Now he had this office job, trying frantically to get to a famous sanatorium in Davos, Switzerland. He would have needed a certain amount of dollars deposited in Switzerland to be accepted. He was not able to go.*

His secretary was a nice-looking young woman, and I was jealous of her. As it turned out, she had a boyfriend. I was relieved. Horst saw me hanging around. He asked me to go for a walk. One did not go on dates. In any case there was nowhere to go. Everything was restricted so we just went for walks. I was sixteen, and he was twenty-one.

We became friends, and he came to talk to my parents. He came to our house, and my parents were so preoccupied with themselves they didn't care. My father had a talk with him and asked him to behave like a gentleman. He did. He told me from the beginning, he was not trying to cheat me, that he had tuberculosis. It was inactive, and he had to take tests regularly. Many times I went with him to the hospital when he took a sputum test, and he told me to take them myself. I always tested negative.

In the beginning of 1941 we heard rumors that Jews had been rounded up for resettlement in the East, that they had been sent to work camps. With this hanging over us we knew it was coming closer. Horst said, "I will not be going to Palestine. I can't get out anymore. So I might as well go with you. Sooner or later, they are going to come for me." His mother lived in eastern Germany. She was taken on another transport. His father was deceased already, so Horst came with us. We had known each other about a year.

Since it had been some time since we had enjoyed any actual freedom of action and movement, news of that type was received with numbness and resignation. As a teenager I felt some excitement. Any change of scenery seemed to be better than to continue to live in our claustrophobic circumstances.

On October 21, 1941 the knock on the door came. Two Gestapo agents arrived early in the morning and told us that we were to be part of a resettlement project to the East. Germany needed Jews to finally do some productive work for the Fatherland that had so long provided for us. "Get ready. You have an hour."

Patiently they allowed us time to pack one suitcase each, as much as we could carry. My mother and grandmother made sure that we took bread and salami, boiled eggs and such. These provisions would later turn out to be a godsend.

I also took a book of poetry by Heinrich Heine with me. He was a German-Jewish poet of whom I was very fond. Many of the best-known German poems and songs were written by him. He converted to Christianity, that way hoping to succeed in contemporary nineteenth-century German society.

We were all marched – parents, grandparents, and my newly acquired boyfriend – to a branch of the Frankfurt railroad station used for freight rather than passenger traffic.

We found many Jewish families sitting on the ground with their luggage piled around them, the last remaining vestige of family integrity. It was clear we had now sunk to a lower level of existence, and the presence of the enemy had become immediate and threatening. SS men in uniform were all around us with dogs and whips. We were ordered to move quickly to our appointed waiting place, and my grandmother stumbled. An SS man kicked her because she did not walk fast enough. It was the first time that I witnessed physical violence. Others had seen it before, but I had never seen it.

We were sitting on that platform for nearly twenty-four hours.

We were subjected to all kinds of bureaucratic procedures, like signing that we voluntarily give up our German citizenship. There was no choice. We had to sign it.

After the war they offered German citizenship back to me. I said, "Not on your life. I never want to be German again! You asked me to give it up, and I don't want it back." I came to the U.S. as a stateless person. They took me anyway. I came under the German quota because I was born there. They couldn't take that away.

I later learned that there were twelve hundred people on that train, old and young, men and women, infants and older children. Of these, I am only one of three, and the only woman, to survive the end of the war.

Deportation

Hundreds of us were tied together with long, heavy ropes, led by these ropes into the wide entrance hall of a freight depot, and then suddenly left there in musty darkness. Among us were screaming children, some tiny and some a little bigger, who held on to whatever piece of clothing they could reach, though it rarely was their mother's. Wedged into the crowd, they were eventually knocked to the ground by some boot.

The old whimper, dragged down by their bags, and the young pant. I stop thinking. The immense weight of my two packages tears my arms out of their sockets. A rucksack sits on my back like an unbearable incubus that pulls me back, and yet I must move on, move on and on. Out of the dark, I hear my mother call my name, and then my father. Voices blend together as they call out names until a strident whistle hacks into the seething of voices. Silence.

The widening glare of a hand-held searchlight plows into the darkness. A voice that reminds you of the rubbing of handcuffs against electric chairs yells, "Pistols at the ready!" In the deadly silence, noisy black boots clatter in perfect time as big, broad fellows in German uniforms heave into sight, their shiny steel helmets emblazoned with shinier death's-heads. Held in big masculine hands, the pistols point all the way around our rope.

The rope pulls us like cattle to the slaughter. Why waste words on us? Right behind me a husky oath, a dull thud, and my grandmother shoots forward on unsteady legs. She has just been shown for the first time that there is no such thing as being unable to move on. "Jew, go on or die!" My grandfather staggers forward. I am young, I am still able to move on, and once again I do not allow myself to think.

The entrance hall opens. A clear night sky stands above us, and the stars are out. To the right the railroad cars are waiting. "Get in, hurry up, hurry up!" Kicks and pushes help us along, and with unbelievable speed eighty people are loaded into one of those ill-designed Polish railroad cars. Packages and luggage are thrown helter-skelter among the people, among the children. The door is locked down, and we wordlessly stare at one another. This is my first inkling that one cannot be polite in a cage. We are all civilized people, but everyone wants a seat.

Only then do I realize, and my heart contracts in sudden panic, that Horst is not with us: my friend, my beloved, my fiancé. All the love my heart could muster has been focused on him, my black-haired twenty-three-year-old boy. Pushing my father away from the window I scream, out of my mind with fear, into the danger-laden night. No answer, only an angry shout, a curse word, comes back out of the dark, and then a short and sharp bang, a warning shot.

Choked with anxiety I fall silent. Both my parents, utterly overwhelmed, began to berate me for my lack of filial love. All else was engulfed by the torment of my consuming worry about Horst – Horst, who for my sake had wordlessly abandoned his own mother in order to follow me into a perilous future.

Fortunately, however, and for this time, my fear was premature. The door of the railroad car was pushed open, and an SS guard shoved him in, my sorely missed friend. As we greeted each other joyfully and rather too exuberantly, the SS man remarked wistfully and sentimentally, "The springtime of young love, if only it stayed so green throughout your life." When someone had the idea of laughing at this, the SS man looked flattered and conceited. As he left the car, he muttered to himself, "After all, not all of them are at fault."

Horst was unbelievably spunky and enterprising. At this point he was trying to show my skeptical and supercilious father how much more his youth and his daredevil energy could accomplish than Father's civilized bourgeois calm. He began by finding ways to get all the scattered luggage out of the way. He made a special point of building a seat for my father under the window, then installed my mother in a corner. He also found seats for the grandparents in a compartment.

After each of the eighty passengers in the railroad car had found some kind of place to sit or squat, all that was left for the two of us was a tiny little spot right next to the toilet. That's where we sat with our legs crossed or, better, pulled in as best we could, for the entire duration of the trip. And it should be added that Horst took over the vital function of regulating the traffic to the toilet. There was less pushing, and people started to behave in a more rational manner.

Throughout the night and the following day that toilet traffic passed more or less carefully over my legs.

At times during the night I leaned against the damp wall of the railroad car as the train rushed eastward. It was becoming increasingly cold. Sleep of course was out of the question, in part because lying down was most uncomfortable and in part because of the "regular" traffic to the toilet.

Across from me lay a woman in her forties, her face covered by a black felt hat that had slipped from her head. I noticed her because unlike most of the others she did not groan and indeed hardly moved as the long, painful hours passed. During the night Horst exchanged a few words with her, but I could not understand them. Only the calm sound of her deep voice affected me pleasantly.

As the night hours slowly ticked away, who knew which towns the train had passed already and who cared. We were robbed of the ability to act and had become marionettes in a horrible spectacle.

The night pressed against the carriage window, velvety black and unconcerned. An iron hand had gripped me, and I dimly sensed that it would lead me, but where and through what I did not know. These, then, were my feelings, and I will not leave them out; after all, my heart was involved. Horst, Horst! I could still smile, for Horst stood between me and the brutal, icy cold of what was happening.

God almighty, all of this could have been foreseen, but who had actually seen it? I know the Germans. I have grown up among them. Of what will they be capable? This was as far as I

could think, too exhausted for more. I reflected for a bit about people, the Jewish people included in this transport and people in general, but I did not come to any conclusion, for I did not really know people.

And at this point I get lost in dreams. Pungent humidity creeps closer and closer to me, the night holds me tightly. There are bags on the ground, bags by the windows, bags around my heart. My fellow human, where are you? Love, where are you? Heaven, where are you? You who hold me between your iron claws, do not shake me too roughly in your scornful game; what good does it do you to see my helpless wriggling?

A wild jerk – the train suddenly jumps backward. Bags tumble about, people tumble about, and my head is violently thrown backward. Half stunned by the impact, I move my neck. By now dawn has penetrated the dark and pours rapidly brightening light into the window. The person across from me notices my groan and sits up, alert. I can soon reassure her that I am not hurt. She is a nurse by profession and obviously wants something to do.

When daylight comes, our faces look gray and show our lack of sleep, and as it gets brighter we are aware of thirst, though for the moment we are not hungry. In one station, where we are strictly forbidden to get out or even look out of the window, Horst again manages to climb out unseen and to bring back some containers filled with highly questionable water. As he hands container after container of it through the window and asks for other vessels to bring more, I experience for the first time a slight foretaste of the greed spawned by utter deprivation.

People make a rush for the containers, and for the first time I hear the groans of satisfied desire, "Water, ah, water!" Dried tongues are pushed out from parched throats. Well-dressed, well-scrubbed, and well-fed people slurp the highly questionable brown liquid. I was able to control myself, and, indeed, the younger people tended to show more starch and toughness than their usually wise and superior elders.

That afternoon we arrived deep in Poland. But there was still no way to find out the exact direction in which we were going since we had no information at all. Several times the train stopped, and then there was anxious speculation about our final destination. Eventually the train stood on a large wooden platform surrounded in the distance by a wooden fence. Rather ragged-looking men with indistinct yellow patches on chest and back eyed us with curiosity. Later they were joined by another cohort of better-dressed men, and it was clear that what they all had on their chests and backs were Stars of David. Speaking a more or less understandable German, they had evasive and quasi-mocking answers to our questions.

Then, loud enough, came the order, "Everybody get out!", and we stopped asking questions. No time for that. We were told to place our luggage on the horse carts that were standing by since we had a several kilometer foot march ahead of us. So Horst and I, wanting to be as comfortable as possible, carried practically nothing with us. As we were herded forward, my mother berated us for acting once again with a lamentable lack of foresight and prudence.

However, as the day wore on, it turned out that the exhausting trip, added to the frightening experiences preceding it, had weakened all of us so much that the smallest piece of luggage became an unbearable burden. So we had our hands full after all, dragging along some of the heavy luggage of both our parents and grandparents.

Surrounded by a heavily armed SS company, we reached a huge wide-open gate bearing the screeching inscription: GHETTO – NO ENTRY, NO EXIT!

Ghetto of Lodz

Our New Environment

Beyond the barbed wire we came upon narrow little streets bogged down in clayey mud. They were lined with ramshackle, filthy stores and tumbledown wooden huts, and broken implements were scattered everywhere. There were heaps of garbage and stunted, low bushes whose naked mutilated branches reached out pitifully. Milling about were people – women, huge numbers of children, skeletons wrapped in rags, barefoot and covered in mud. They all stared enviously at us adequately, even well-dressed newcomers, and their eyes seemed to suck every last piece of clothing off our backs.

I sensed their glances. I felt sick, and I asked one of the adolescent skeletons for a drink of water. He brought me some greasy liquid in a disgustingly dirty cup, but I was so parched with thirst that I swallowed it without looking.

There may have been fifty or more little children, urchins – hungry, dirty, with dilapidated clothes who all had little tin cups with a spoon. They banged them to ask us for food because we looked well fed. We had whatever food was left from the train, and I remember my mother had a piece of salami that she gave to a couple of kids. These were the children of people who had no resources. So they were the ones who were most vulnerable.

From the beginning, I could see the children in the streets were starving. There were telltale signs. Their faces were bloated, swollen under their eyes, and their fingers were starting to swell. Eventually the belly swells, but the first thing was always around the eyes. Once you got that far, you knew you did not have long to live. From the moment we marched into the ghetto, it was pretty clear that a lot of people were dying, particularly the children. They and all the old people were very, very poorly nourished. We didn't have any food for the children.

The ghetto was established in 1939. As soon as the Germans entered Poland, they set up ghettos all over the place. The Nazis picked the most decrepit and dirtiest section of Lodz. Lodz had a very large population of Jews, several hundred thousand. There were German colonies in Poland from a long time ago. They *were part of the local population. When Hitler came to power, they suddenly rediscovered their German heritage, and they immediately became allies of the winning power. They became two hundred percent German, and the Germans relied on them. They put them right around the ghetto so that in Lodz, different from Warsaw, there was very little interaction between the Polish population and the ghetto population. People who might have had friends outside the ghetto walls could not get through there because these local Germans took their jobs very seriously.*

The Germans renamed Lodz. They called it Litzmannstadt after a German general from the First World War who became a Nazi. Many people had been in the ghetto for almost two years, and many others had already been shipped out, either to a work camp or to Chelmno, an extermination camp not far from Lodz.

After a seemingly unending trek through the morass of these streets and through unending scenes of misery such as I had never seen before, we finally arrived in front of a fairly large building, a former school. The open gate of the courtyard slowly swallowed up the incoming procession of twelve hundred persons. Spreading throughout the courtyard as an indistinct black throng, this mass slowly pushed its way into the building, pushed as well by those in the rear. A troop of the men who had received us at the railroad stop was yelling and jumping all around us. No one could or even wanted to understand them very well. By now we had learned that they were members of a kind of Ghetto Police.

Horst, his power of initiative still undiminished, had approached one of them to ask some questions; it was a well-dressed, good-looking youngish man in a visored cap showing a tin badge with a number topped by a star. He wore a yellow and white armband showing the same number and the same star. He introduced himself with barely concealed self-importance as a sergeant in the "security services," in other words, the Ghetto Police.

I noticed that all these men wore similar kinds of badges. The sergeant went on to tell us that he spoke four languages and would have told us a lot more if our attention had not obviously faltered.

For during this short halt almost all of the people from our train had entered the building, and we were among the very last still outside. When, to our dismay, we realized this, we tried to catch up by pushing our way in. But it was impossible, for the tightly packed crowd spilled all the way out into the courtyard, so that in the end we simply had to wait for about an hour for the first onslaught to subside. When we were finally able to squeeze into one of the upper stories, it turned out that the larger rooms were already so full that we could see nothing but the swaying of a teeming black mass of people. We could hear nothing but a jumble of grunting and screeching voices, a noise that tore at the ears and the nerves.

The men of the security service were yelling helplessly as they pointlessly waved their rubber nightsticks in the air. They did not know us well enough yet to make use of them against us. There were some among us, especially among the young men, who were quite attracted to the idea of "systematic organization for the public good." After all, many of them, including Horst, had for many years absorbed high-falutin notions of "solidarity, productive work, and spiritual loyalty" in the youth centers of the Zionist Organization.

Meanwhile the chaos in the different rooms had abated at least to the extent that one could distinguish between luggage and people. Shortly thereafter we received an order from somebody who at the time was still a most mysterious figure to us, Chaim Rumkowski, the "Eldest of the Jews of Litzmannstadt," who we soon learned was habitually referred to as the "Praeses." Half of the resettled newcomers were to be moved to a house in an adjoining street. This meant that "only" about six hundred persons were left in the first building.

By now night had fallen. We were dead tired and simply lay down wherever we happened to be standing. Here too there was considerable pushing, yelling, and stamping of feet. The weightiest question was whether legs should be placed parallel to or between those of the neighbor. Bourgeois manners having already faded considerably, everyone tried in complete selfishness to place his/her extremities on top of the next person's rather than being burdened by them.

My grandparents, normally a most affectionate couple, were fighting over a briefcase that would have been wide enough to serve as a pillow for both their heads. I no longer remember who won that fight. Youth took me into its tender arms, and I soon went to sleep. During the night I was startled by renewed clattering and stamping of feet. Coffee was brought in. A huge dirty kettle was placed by the door, and a fat girl in a grayish white apron ladled the liquid into the cups. In the midst of this operation the light went out, and renewed screaming broke out. Some people had been scalded by the burning hot liquid, some had been kicked, some had lost their old sleeping place and tried to find a new one on top of someone else.

This went on until a gray, wan morning dawned. One could have cut the air in the overcrowded room with a knife. The warmth of all these bodies melded into the fine dampness of late autumn. Moreover, we were covered with a crust of dust and dirt, for we had not yet found a place to wash.

Soon my mother began to complain that she could not stand to be in the crush of this crowd. So Horst set out to look for a better place, returning in discouragement before too long. All he had been able to find was one small free area in a hallway, but Mother was willing to put up with anything for a little breath of fresher air, so we dragged our stuff to the new place.

Later we found a faucet supplying a little trickle of water in a neighboring courtyard and felt no embarrassment at stripping as far as possible and washing in the presence of the speechlessly gaping locals. Returning to our encampment upstairs, we found Mother, shivering and crouching miserably on some knapsack. Her lips purple and with tears running down her cheeks, she kept muttering, "Oh if only I had something to do, anything to do." At home Mother could always find useful – and sometimes useless – things to keep her occupied. Idleness, especially in these conditions, was unbearable to her.

I could do nothing to comfort her. In fact I was rather provoked and beginning to feel a choking sensation. Horst's smile too was becoming less steady. I felt a great desire to quarrel. A steady stream of local Jews showed up to gape at us. Many of them, the poorly dressed ones, contented themselves with letting their eyes roam freely over our belongings.

The better-dressed ones involved us in endless conversations about the political situation in Germany and our opinions concerning the duration of the war. We admitted that we considered ourselves poorly informed, whereupon our visitors explained to us with superior smiles that within a month the Nazi-action – here they pointedly touched their necks – would be completely over. Didn't we know how far the Russian forces had advanced in the East? No, we had no idea. All we had heard was some vague news about the fighting at Stalingrad. Stalingrad! Don't be ridiculous! We are talking Warsaw here, Warsaw! And how far is Warsaw from here? Warsaw? Well, something like two hundred kilometers. This happy surprise made our hearts skip a beat. The deep conviction with which this information was imparted took our breath away. It almost crushed us.

After a while a young girl came up the stairs. She attracted my attention by the youthfulness of her movements – the rest of our visitors, though young enough in years, seemed strangely elderly in their movements and their whole demeanor. This girl, sturdily built and blond-haired, was dressed in simple and clean clothes. She immediately pounced on me with an overly enthusiastic greeting in pure high German. I found out right away that, born in Breslau [now Wroclaw], she had been expelled in the course of the action of late 1938, when all Polish citizens had been transported to Poland, ending up here after being shuttled about here and there.

She was the first one to tell me, "I have been in the ghetto for two long years." Two years! Once again, my heart skipped a beat, but this time from dismay. "Why, we were just told that our liberation was at hand – after the tremendous advance of the fighting forces. The people here are amazingly well-informed." She smiled an oddly unpleasant smile. "That's what they have been saying for the last two years." My eyes opened wide in astonishment: "But they seemed so convinced of what they reported. How else could they spread such dangerous propaganda based on absurd hopes?" The girl, in angry indignation: "Of course they believe it – I too believe it – how

else would we be able to live?" Looking pityingly from me to her brother, who had meanwhile joined us, she said, "What a *yeke* she is!," using the slang word used by the Polish Jews for German Jews.

Suddenly a door opened across the hall; I had not even noticed it. The bright light of a lamp could be seen, tables with pretty, colorful tablecloths, cupboards and a neatly made bed – a stream of hominess and warmth poured out of that half-opened door. A strange yearning pulled at my heart. Three days, and already a world seemed to lie between me and that sight. Two ladies hurried by, avoiding the sight of us with the determined squeamishness, the kind of overly cautious movements a woman might affect when she must jump over a puddle wearing an extremely expensive gown. They were dressed carefully and warmly, and I noticed the two silk stars they wore, neatly attached, front and back. Dark veils came down from their hats, covering the upper part of the faces. But I did see their mouths, dark red and heart-shaped. Once again I spontaneously blurted out, "Aren't they Jews?"

I had to put up with Ruth's, my new acquaintance's, mocking glance and her painfully unpleasant smile. "When you have gotten to where they are, you will no longer need news, you can live without it. One of them cooks for the Chief, the Eldest of the Jews. That kind of job is not for the likes of us. I am dragging my feet – and while I no longer give much of a damn about anything, I still give a damn about myself. I don't know how it will go – my father is already starving. He yells, and my brother yells, and my mother cries – I know what she wants me to do when she looks at me with red-rimmed eyes. My boss is young, a favorite of the Chief, he is lacking nothing."

Suddenly she cries out hysterically, "But I'm not ready yet, no, I'm not ready!" and runs off.

Slowly I wander back to my mother, eager to learn and curious, feeling superior but also deeply humiliated. Mother is still hunched down in the same place, weepy and old. I should caress her, but I can't comfort her. Stock-still and absent-mindedly, I stare down at her until she covers her face with her hands and begins to sob soundlessly. Further down in the hallway I run into Horst, who asks me to give him some bread for friends who had brought very few supplies from home. We are not yet hungry, and so I hand over the bread without hesitation.

In the evening we again spread blankets on the floor and lay down. By now others as well had settled in our corner, and this was really the first time that I distinguished individuals within the revolting mass phenomenon of the forced resettlement. There was, for instance, a pretty, round woman, whom I noticed because of her very lively black eyes over which she kept batting fluttering lids. She had immediately set up her dainty little hatbox in a corner and began, charmingly and unselfconsciously, to concentrate on waving her long dark hair. Then she spread a little colorful silk scarf over a box and looked with coquettish pleasure at the domestic space she had created. Her behavior amused me and made me feel a little better, and Horst too had made friends with her right away.

Normally both of us, Horst as well as I, hated coquetry. But in this case, its irrepressible staying power was somehow refreshing. Raw nature with its smell of decay had already touched us too closely. The young woman's husband was tall and ungainly and wore glasses. This last characteristic seemed oddly important – it was actually the only thing I noticed about him – for even in his tender love for Ilse (that was his wife's name), he was nothing more than her husband. As my father put it, not very cleverly but accurately: "Mr. Ilse."

Our other neighbor attracted my attention only when it was already dark, for he never stopped telling more or less funny jokes. We laughed. The next morning I saw that he was a wretched little cripple. But that evening we laughed again.

The following day Horst and I went into the ghetto for the first time. The rain came down between the roofs in monotonous stripes. The sky was invisible; there was only steaming grayness to which one did not dare lift one's eyes.

Soon an oddly bawling sing-song creeps into our ears – gray and monotonous like this fading November day and at the same time alien and unfathomable like the yearning of Asia caught in the barbed wires of misery, "*Papyrosse* [Cigarettes] –

Saccharine! *Papyrosse*! Toffee, ten for five, toffee, red and yellow toffee!"

It was a simple rising and falling melody with which half-grown, raggedy children hawked their wares. For hours on end they stood motionless on a corner, unconcerned about the cold and the fine mist of rain. Big eyes staring out of yellowish-pale faces restlessly darted about in feverish eagerness to snap up a little something at every miserable opportunity.

They were motionless as their lean, dirty, clammy hands offered dubious sweets, saccharine, cigarettes only half filled with smelly weeds. "*Papyrosse*! Saccharine! *Papyrosse!*"

We entered a "pub" full of dingy tables where persons of both sexes were loitering. Sitting in a booth in the back was a group of men in traditional Jewish garb, with caftans and side-locks, but all ragged and sticky with filth. Gesticulating wildly, they screeched at the top of their voices. Suddenly one of them stood up furiously and left the room, while another sent indignant laughter after him.

In another area of the pub sat a group of young men, members of the security service; they were called "Ghetto Police." While they were not wearing side-locks, they were unshaven and acted boisterously, telling silly jokes and reacting with inappropriately loud guffaws.

We ordered a bowl of soup; it was a weird red broth with bits of stuff floating in it. The color somehow had a frightening effect on me. I found it painfully suggestive, to the point that when I made a heroic effort to taste it, I could not dispel the thought of blood. So I stopped eating and could only wonder at the positively irrepressible appetite with which all the others wolfed down the disgusting slop.

Outside, I felt crushed by the milling crowds in the narrow streets. Women slipped out of dark archways, the fringes of their big shawls dragging in the mud and children peeking from every side of their skirts.

Standing or crouching in the doorways, as well as in the middle of the streets, hucksters carrying glass-covered cases hanging from straps over their shoulders remained motionless for hours on end as they offered their small wares for sale. In some places bread and root vegetables were for sale, for the most part big white radishes, turnips, rutabagas, and sometimes beets.

Prices were unjustifiably high. This was not surprising to people who had experience, a category that did not include us. A two-kilo loaf of bread cost about seven ghetto-marks, a currency issued for the ghetto and supposedly equal to the German mark, but printed in the ghetto and bearing the picture and the signature of the Eldest of the Jews.

A kilo of potatoes sold for seventy pfennig. Prices were stable only as long as supplies came in. A gauge for the state of the food market – and it was just about the only one – was the sale price at any given moment for saccharine. Like other inferior nonessentials, saccharine was supplied by smugglers. At the time, twenty saccharine tablets cost sixteen pfennig; at the height of the famine, the price rose to fifty pfennig for one tablet.

In the course of the day, we decided and actually proceeded to elect a chairman who would represent the interests of our transport's community in its relations with the internal and external ghetto authorities. He was expected to maintain, or indeed create, as much order as possible in the internal affairs of the community.

As for the person of this chairman, it is sufficient to say that he was the former head of the Jewish community of Frankfurt, a middle-aged man of pale, well-groomed, hanging-cheeked plumpness, the very picture, painted a thousand times, of a robust chairman-of-the board type who had financially and morally clawed his way to the top ever since his un-youthful youth.

I knew his wife, a person with pale-blue eyes and perfect makeup. She used to live in an elegant apartment in the western section of Frankfurt. Now she exhibited an air of tragic heroism between the deeply pulled down veil of her hat and the raised high collar of her fur coat. She now "resided" amidst

"only" twenty persons, "close acquaintances" of hers who had given her the brightest and most comfortable corner of the room. This allowed her to stretch out her extremities side by side without interference and distinguished her from the mass of those of us who were "chaired." It provided the outward sign that she was indeed the wife of the chairman.

Other former leaders of the Jewish community were also elected to enlarge the circle of leadership. The first action of this board was to comply with an order received from the ghetto administration that a certain number of younger, healthy men were to be made available for a labor transport to Poznan.

I was much afraid that this would mean that Horst would be separated from me after all, and I was feverishly looking for a way out. Having heard reports of various unofficial announcements, we decided to declare ourselves "officially engaged to be married." Since the rule was that married people or others with family responsibilities were not to be considered, and since we also had a medical certificate, we were able to avoid a separation.

On this occasion the sturdiest and nicest fellows were separated from us, never to be seen again. It soon turned out that there was no one without family responsibilities, and so this rule too was disregarded. Sons were torn from their parents, husbands from their wives, and fathers from their children. Many of Horst's friends were among them, and we all kissed when we took leave from each other.

On that gloomy November evening the chairman stood by, earnest and important, surrounded by a group of Ghetto Police. A first snow had fallen and was melting into the damp mud as our friends were led away.

Suffering of the Newcomers

New transports came from Czechoslovakia and many other countries, not just from Germany. However, it is as if we German Jews had never existed there, at least it seems that way in the surviving archival records of the ghetto. Such were the interior politics of the ghetto.

We were not only oppressed by the Germans, but there was a secondary oppression. Psychologically things became more and more complicated. I have a resistance to telling about it because it implicates a lot of people. It implicates oneself. One would like to say everybody was pure and honest and wonderful, but that was not so. There were people who were pure and honest and wonderful. They were a minority, even among the Jews. It is like walking to the abyss and looking down into one's own nature, into human nature, and that can be a horrible thing to realize. Every human being can do that.

I ought to explain something about the ghetto administration. The man who was put in charge was Chaim Rumkowski. He was a nobody before the war. He had been the head of an orphanage. He got to know the German commander in charge of the whole area and was appointed by him. He, a thoroughly corrupt individual, was now in charge. There was a whole group around him who wanted to get as much personal gain out of it as they could.

The Germans promised everything to Rumkowski. "Your people will be fine," they said, and he believed them. I mean how stupid can you be! He thought that he had something going with them. He thought that with a Yiddishe kop (a Jewish brain) he could outsmart the Germans. That turned out to be not so simple.

One thing he was able to finagle. He said, "If you give us more food, you can put factories here. I'll deliver the labor if you give us additional food." And for a while they did that. Without the work provided inside the ghetto, they would have had no reason to keep us alive at all. So they did put certain factories in there. We made uniforms for the army. Rags were torn up, then braided for us to sew to make into slippers. There was also a metal factory. I ended up working in the uniform factory, even though I had never sewn on a sewing machine in my life. The electric sewing machine was a heavy sewing machine, huge. One can learn everything if one has to. We got an extra ration.

We were given rations every two weeks which consisted of a little brown sugar, a small loaf of bread, a can of horse meat, and a couple of other things. There was no fat, no eggs or anything. Of course, unfortunately, people devoured them as soon as they got them and then had to go around hungry the rest of the time. For certain jobs, one might get additional soup, which was generally thicker at work.

We German Jews didn't know of these things. We were not offered work for quite a long time, and people died unbelievably quickly. You could just look at them, and they were dying within weeks. They had absolutely no resources, and nobody told us about resources. They died very quickly.

German Jews came from a different background. Our self-esteem was so low. We were unable to adjust psychologically to ghetto conditions, unlike the Polish Jews. We had no way to move into positions of influence, and so we suffered the most and perished at an alarming rate. Virtually no one survived from that group.

Some of the fellows from the Frankfurt transport, who had remained behind in the Lodz ghetto, now tried to get work, any kind of work. The long dull days and the even longer and duller evenings of hanging around in the overcrowded rooms had a devastating effect on their nerves and their moods. Furthermore, a crushing need for money soon became dangerously obvious. When we were expelled, we were not allowed to take along more than one hundred marks per person. Following a few spot checks successfully carried out by the German authorities, some examples were made in such a fashion that no one was interested in further derring-do. The provisions we had brought from home had, of course, been consumed before very long, so that we already had to buy almost everything we needed at black-market prices. All we received legally was three hundred grams of dry bread a day and a daily soup whose ingredients and filthy presentation made it inedible.

I had an acquaintance. Both of us were not yet eighteen at the time. Her husband had been amazingly quick to get a job with the security force. Although he was only given night duty, his standing in our community had risen considerably. Even the board members took approving notice of this ambitious young man. After all, his remarkable rise had come about by the grace of the Ghetto Chief and some of the long-standing inhabitants.

Horst too was impressed by this development, and he became very upset and agitated. But I did not ask him about the reason. I did not want to ask, for the oppressive atmosphere of overly close togetherness stifled my sensibilities, deprived my feelings of oxygen, as it were.

I sensed that both of us avoided even a few minutes of being alone together, which in the past had seemed too short. As time went on, every small show of affection was given in haste and embarrassment, so that we soon stopped them altogether. I tried, at least, to be ashamed of this cooling of our relationship, for I saw that Horst was wasting away. After trying to change over to compassion, I ended up taking refuge in memories.

The only result of these pitiful experiments was distaste and coldness. Sometimes I seethed with silent anger that they had shorn off his thick black hair, that worry had caused his deep, sentimental, dark blue eyes to become pale, and that he looked terribly sad when he furtively glanced at his beloved musical instruments, several harmonicas and flutes. I often urged him to play them, but he would only look at me sadly and say, "How about you, why aren't you writing?" To that I had no answer, and so I would angrily stalk off.

One evening all able-bodied men were ordered to Radegast station, the loading platform in Marysin, to unload railroad cars. My father and Horst were included in this group. It stormed and rained all night long, but my mother and I slept reasonably well, probably better than usual, for in the absence of the men there was more room for us. Our crippled neighbor was telling his jokes as usual. We laughed loudly, and our neighbor Ilse put on a white blouse before she snuggled down between the thin blankets with her "Hänschen," whose name was really Max.

The next morning our two men returned soaked through, exhausted, and hungry. I eagerly cut off a few thick slices of bread for them. I was amazed and distressed by the indifference with which Horst wolfed down the hard, black crusts. Mother and I left the blankets to make room for the two men. But there was no other place for us in the room, and so I went to one of the other dormitories to talk to some acquaintances.

The younger people sat around on knapsacks or on the floor. The girls were combing their hair, putting on makeup, or mending something. The fellows were reporting on political news they had picked up, complete with hair-splitting commentaries of their own. After they had exhausted this subject, they just stared at each other wordlessly. Never have I seen duller, and at the same time, more deeply probing glances than those exchanged in these circumstances of being mentally and physically at bay.

Then they turned to dirty jokes for a while. I listened to both themes with a troubled detachment tinged with a certain excitement, and so, I believe, did the other girls present. Only the young woman whose husband worked the night shift for the security service was nervously attentive as she sat there next to her sleeping husband.

Later she saw me to the door and told me about her older sister's husband, a completely worthless fellow who had not yet found a job and had even gotten out of pushing railroad cars at Marysin that night. I thought of my father and Horst, and anger once again constricted my throat. I quickly moved away and returned to our corner.

My father lay there, already awake and very pale. He motioned me to him and told me that as he was working that night he was noticed by an engineer of the ghetto's "vegetable administration" for his care and expertise in loading and shipping the raw vegetables. When they engaged in conversation, the man had again admired his expert work and then had promised to help him get a job in his department. "Then I will see to it that we have enough to eat. Then it will become clear that a mature, serious man still commands more sense of responsibility and know-how than some green dreamer and talker who folds right away at the first blast of rough wind, when it is up to him to take care of his people. Besides, I have six years of military service behind me. That's what it takes to make a man."

Horst was still sleeping, or at least his eyes were closed. At this moment he was close to my heart, and I hated my father. My father's intelligent brown eyes – I knew how much I resembled him – intently looked at me, and I sensed how much he missed my faraway sister right now. And at the same time I was also aware that the thought of her pulled me away from Horst, all of which overwhelmed me with a furious anguish that hurled me into utter hopelessness and then suddenly subsided, leaving me in a state of dull mindlessness.

I hardly noticed that Horst had gone out into the ghetto. When he returned, I was frightened by the very calm look on his face. He took me aside with a gesture of humble tenderness. I was seized by an unspeakable fear that he would speak loving words that were in his heart, loving words to which my lips and my heart were unable to respond. And yet he was closer to me than anyone else, closer than my father and my mother.

But what he said was this: "Do you want me to become a cad? Do you want me to sell the dreams we share so that I can lick some grub from the dog shit? Do you want me to go to the sanctuary of the traitors to beg for a kick that will push me into one of their heated side rooms? If you want me to, I will toss my flute into the latrine, duck my head, and look proud to join the gang.

Perhaps that would be best, for then all the proper people, including your father, would consider me ready for marriage, responsible and able to plan ahead, and perhaps I would also escape starvation, which I feel creeping closer. But if you don't want it, I may well be thrown to the swine, but I won't be a swine myself. Then you will be the one to destroy my flute when it no longer serves a purpose."

I looked straight into his eyes, saw them deep blue and sentimental for the last time, and said, "I don't want it!" And so Horst did not become a policeman, and my father despised him for it. As a result he became more and more pale every day and often asked me in a gruff voice to put the bread away quickly, to avoid a disaster. By "disaster" he meant that otherwise he would eat it all in one sitting. My mother too ate her slice of bread more and more quickly every day, and she followed it with smoldering, long, and greedy glances when the loaf had to be put back into the suitcase. Father and I were better able to keep our eyes and our feelings under control.

I don't know when it was that I began to consider bread an incredible delicacy, but I do know that as time went on, eating it became a pleasure such as I had never experienced before. I soon began to savor every bite with great intensity. The increasing shortage demanded most careful and measured husbanding on our part. Initially this new situation was more pleasurable than frightening, but later, even before I experienced physically painful and damaging hunger, it led to a cramped and perverse holding back that is common when natural pleasures are exaggerated in one direction or another. In this case it showed itself in excessively slow eating, in the effort to suck enjoyment from every bite, or else in an overwhelming gluttony that must devour whatever is available to its greed and is unable to think of a tomorrow.

I suppose my father and I fell into the first category, my mother and Horst into the second. Meanwhile Horst, constantly irritated by my father's barbed words and glances and my mother's nervous scolding, continued his desperate search for some kind of work.

Father, despite the promises of Mr. "Engineer" – a title that, oddly enough, was claimed by about half the population – had not yet been asked to accept a position in the vegetable department.

One day Horst came in beaming. He was to be employed in a carpentry shop. Having braved rain and frost to stand in line at the door of the employment office, he obtained a registration form for taking an entrance examination for the carpentry shop.

He passed and was overjoyed. After all, he was one of the first in our transport to find work. I should add that my father refused to react to this new state of affairs with even a glance. The strength of my father's personality was such that his glances were more powerful than his words. And he felt that he had the right and the obligation to dampen the triumphal enthusiasm of us women with a special little gesture of his hands or a special little smile.

Horst went to work, and every morning I felt justified in cutting off an extra large piece of the communal loaf of bread for him. At work they dished out a bowl of hot rutabaga soup at noon. Originally the feeling of triumph about his success in finding work restored Horst's former forceful demeanor. But soon the unaccustomed exertion and the inferior and insufficient diet caused him increasing exhaustion, continual weight loss, and steadily worsening hunger.

He exaggerated a proletarian lack of manners that was most unbecoming to him. He pointedly avoided looking at my parents and even demanded certain rights to which he felt entitled by dint of "heroism and success" but which, however wrong this may be, only come with the familiarity of biological kinship.

I could see how others were wrong, but after a while I came to see that I too was wrong. This reassured me somewhat but at the same time aroused strong feelings of disdain and discouragement in me, for I understood that there is no normal way to overcome human degradation. And I felt too weak against this enormity. I knew the path only too well. It was carved with an iron spade through the most chaotic and fallow denigration of life, and the final decree, one way or another, is out of our hands.

Before long my father succeeded in obtaining the promised job in the vegetable department. On the very first day he told us that he was in a position to eat all the rutabagas he wanted and brought home a batch to prove it. Horst kept quiet, but I could see how much it hurt him that his work did not contribute to keeping us alive.

Soon my father was given a yellow and white armband stamped with the name of his department; it certified him as an official of the "Eldest of the Jews in the Litzmannstadt Ghetto." In the beginning he wore it with pride as the badge of his special position within the ghetto community. But soon he became indifferent to it, and in the end he positively hated it.

My father's new position had the result that before long we were given a place by the window in a room holding twenty-two persons, which allowed us to enlarge our "*Lebensraum*" (living space) to the extent of using suitcases, knapsacks, and blankets to construct a kind of couch for our daytime use. Ilse Frohmann with all her relatives – husband, parents-in-law, sister-in-law, one of her husband's cousins and her husband – also moved into the room with us.

Meanwhile we had sufficiently explored the nearby areas of the ghetto to find out about some so-called gas kitchens. As the name indicated, these were kitchens in which ten to thirteen gas burners, in some cases gas cookers, were mounted on wooden or steel frames. A woman cashier gave out numbers corresponding to one of the burners and collected the fees. Normally the price for one hour of cooking was thirty pfennig.

Because of the horrendous coal shortage before the onset of winter, everyone who had anything to cook could take it to a gas kitchen. For the resettled newcomers, whose extremely limited living space created very special conditions, these kitchens represented a considerable benefit. After all, we were not even able to get hold of more than a few drops of hot water or even coffee on our own.

Little things, normally too unimportant to be noticed at all, turned into insolvable problems in our circumstances. Every drop of hot water, every scrap of firewood could only be acquired at exorbitant prices. Meanwhile the price of saccharine went up every day, and bread had reached about sixteen marks.

So we had to put up with sitting around for hours on end in one of these overcrowded gas kitchens whenever we wanted to cook the rutabagas Father brought back. Yet for many people, including myself, I admit the gas kitchen was a place where one could be nice and warm for a few hours and where, moreover, the diversity of the many people who kept coming and going all the time provided a welcome change from the wearying monotony of life in the transit camps with their heart-rending sights of steadily increasing misery.

Half-grown children, exhibiting an aged seriousness common to those marked by early hunger, were stirring the steaming pots. Sometimes they would fish out a potato and chew it noisily, which gave them the forbidden thrill, well known to the psychology of hunger, of having snatched an extra bite from the rest of their family.

The cashier here is a goddess, whose favor is courted by all who enter the premises. If she wants – that is to say, if you are able to pay her for it – she can move you close to the head of the line or, as the case may be, further back. Instinctively I sometimes felt that there could not be a more desirable goal than to be a cashier in one of these gas kitchens.

The ghetto had no generations. Children and older adults had few physical reserves to fight against hunger and disease. The population consisted of the survivors even during the years of the existence of the ghettos and camps. Just as some people seem to be genetically programmed to resist or survive cancer, so were there people who were made to resist successfully the onslaught of starvation and infectious diseases. The selections carried out by the Germans were helped by the inborn molecule of death and self-destruction.

We were all young in the ghetto, but we didn't look it. Our physiognomies were ageless. There were wild, unfocussed eyes, silent, indrawn lips, and haggardness around the cheek and neck … only defined and exaggerated by hunger.

Although we had birthdays, the days were marked more by wonderment at actual time passing than by feelings of celebration. Time passed, on the other hand, was also a cold flush of victory over the enemy who was out to destroy us, the triumph of having lived another day, another month, another year.

The ghetto had no fast days, as it had no days that marked events, historical, religious or personal. If a day was remembered, if a calendar intruded into the consciousness at all, it was registered with surprise. Surprise that time with the usual subdivisions of seconds, minutes, hours, days, weeks, months, and years was going on, somewhere out there in the world of "normalcy," when we had long thought that it had come to a standstill, or was grinding very slowly, revolving in our dried-out guts, around our hanging flesh and our dirty rags.

On an utterly dreary morning, the order came: "Line up the entire Collective!" In our case, this referred to all the people who came together on the transport from Frankfurt.

The many leaders and mini-leaders of our complex and absurd organization were rushing around in breathless eagerness. The task at hand was to plant this thousand-headed horde of starving women and children, a hideous conglomeration of swollen limbs – are they humans, are they animals? You decide, Mr. Puppeteer! – in neatly circled rows. Rows of five – it was the first but by no means the last time it was done.

How our feet dragged the mud. Dragged it, pulled it up, dragged it. Some looked up to the sky, not for the first but perhaps for the last time!

Horst lay on his rags, burning with fever, burning up. I knew that. I too stared up to the sky – not for the last time, but I did not know that.

It was gray, this sky. Nothing unusual about that. Everyone knows a gray sky or many gray skies. They are pretty unimportant, but they do lower the mood, as the saying goes. At the time I did not think about this. I believe I did not think at all. I stared into the sky: gray and unimportant, gray and unimportant. I was eighteen years old.

"The whole Collective, line up!"

I wondered how they could muster this decisiveness, this staunchness, these clipped military orders. They too were hungry. I knew that, and I was glad. They too had become yellow larvae, puppets – hi-ho, Mr. Puppeteer! Oh you ridiculous leaders and mini-leaders!

We were marching. Stumbling along next to me was a little girl, a nine-year-old with pale brown eyes. I held her hand until she walked steadily. My mother walked by my side. She was stepping firmly, as if she were "free" at home and off to the haying, carrying a rake on her shoulder. My smile must have been mocking, for she pinched her lips and tightened the strings of her gray knitted hood.

Thus, we walked a long way across the bridge, through the ghetto's tenacious mud, a thousand of us in a row. On the way we ran into small groups of officiously galloping Ghetto Police belonging to the so-called Special Section of the Guardians of Public Order (*Sonderabteilung des Ordnungsdienstes*). They were wearing smart dark gray uniforms with neatly stitched, brand-new Stars of David.

Some timid questions about "Why" and "Where" were hesitatingly thrown out to the self-assured uniformed men as they rushed by. "Rumkowski, the Praeses, says so," came the mocking answer and we fell silent. Thereafter nobody asked any more questions – we just kept marching.

We were led to a huge square, an open space. We were lined up. Nor were we the only transport Collective that was being "lined up." All the right angles of the square were filled with dark groups of people.

It was an old square, an old Polish square in a Polish town. To be sure, this was the ugliest part of town, the criminal neighborhood probably, but this square was above all austere and old. To the left, behind the Cologne Collective, there may once have been a bazaar. It had a wide entrance with a wrought-iron gate under a crumbling archway. Old and austere it was. To the right a few low-slung houses, turning their backs to us in embarrassment. They were inconspicuous – grey and tired like everything else.

And also, there was a crucifix there.

Crucifixes shouldn't mean much to me; I am a Jew and sympathetic after all to the teachings of Moses. No, I admit, none of this went through my mind at the time – for we were gathered around a gallows.

Do Not Forgive Them

Well now, Jesus up there on the cross:
Carved like this in rough, dirty stone,
I have seen you a hundred, a thousand times.
Listen Jesus, you, up there, there on the cross,
Do you hear, do you hear?
What do you make of that gallows,
That gallows for your brother, your brother!
The one who will hang there, you know,
He is not that poor thief whose sin
You had to take away by your love.
No, no, Jew Jesus, the one they'll hang there
He is your brother, your brother in spirit and flesh.
But Father, do not forgive them,
For they know very well what they do!

The Jew Jesus there on the cross bows his head, as he has bowed it for a thousand years – but it seems to me that now he bows it a little more. As if a great burden had been added to the great burdens he has borne for a thousand years.

So, that's a gallows in our midst. Perhaps I saw it right away when we came to the square. Somebody says, "How about that, a gallows, the Praeses says so. Ha ha ha." Perhaps it was I, perhaps someone else. We are damnably jocular these days, full of mockery, belligerent. "Ha, ha!, a gallows, the Praeses says so. Hi-ho, Mr. Puppeteer!"

A kind of play car draws up – a baby blue limousine, a slender limousine – yes, it really is a play limousine. Six green uniforms get out plus two submachine guns. Six death's-heads and six pairs of shiny boots. The two submachine guns point at the crowd lined up in the square, turning this way and that, that way and this. They keep us in check.

A weird chess game that checks the pawns with submachine guns. The other four are smoking cigarettes, even enjoying them, blowing smoke at each other; they also smile and play with the gold on their pudgy fingers. While they are having this very casual, almost off-duty conversation, one of them snaps his thumb and forefinger at the earnestly waiting Ghetto Police.

One morning I noticed that one of the girls living in the room with us – she was one of the two daughters (nineteen and twenty years old) of a woman whose husband had disappeared into the Buchenwald Concentration Camp long ago – seemed unusually disturbed as she was combing her hair. Soon after she confided to me that she had found a louse in her hair. She begged me to tell her of a way to deal with this new calamity. Unfortunately I knew nothing about this, and so I could only advise her to go to one of the older nurses who might know what to do. And for once my advice was correct.

From this day on, a big old nurse, whose feet were so swollen from arthritis that she was unable to leave her room, spent all her time applying de-lousing caps and sapodilla vinegar.

But alas, once it had started, the scourge continued to spread, eventually infesting even our clothing. It was only brought under control when we were distributed into smaller residential units. An official de-lousing facility did not exist in the ghetto.

Before long, of course, all different kinds of typhus became quite common; not surprisingly, typhoid fever was most prevalent.

Here are some particulars. In our room the situation soon looked like this: Approximately the size of an average living room, it was inhabited by twenty-two persons. In the beginning we – especially Ilse, who by dint of her looks, her decisive manner, and her much appreciated professional skill as a nurse seemed to be most likely to succeed – had tried to negotiate a reduction of this number. But we failed and were handed an edict to the effect that we were to "cease and desist making further efforts to reduce the established number by various kinds of inappropriate shenanigans, to accept the unfortunate but unchangeable conditions, and to obey the orders of the transport authorities."

However, thanks to my mother's restless activity, the room was wet-mopped at least once a day. For the fact is that people had fallen prey to a repellent indifference that went far beyond the resignation that was necessary and beneficial under these conditions.

As I realized from the outset, the oldest persons – those who had spent a lifetime in normal and tranquil circumstances – were the ones who would hunker down for hours and days in the same place without moving, without thinking, who would hungrily and without stopping wolf down the food they were handed and then greedily watch their neighbor who had eaten more slowly and therefore had a few spoonfuls of soup left.

Soon most of them did not have the energy to get up after eating to wash out their pots – plates, of course, had become a thing of the past. Given the extreme difficulty in getting washed – a washbowl remained an unaffordable luxury – and the horrendous condition of the toilet facilities, where a special technique was needed to enter a latrine at all, it was no wonder that living conditions and the health of the inmates deteriorated from day to day.

Since, moreover, we continued to sleep on the drafty floor and to live on unwholesome and mostly liquid food, we came down one by one with unending bladder troubles. And that was the beginning of a tragicomedy. It became almost impossible to sleep at night and thus to forget our misery for a few hours. There was constant coming and going throughout the long night hours, and there always seemed to be somebody hovering above or even stepping on the sleeper's limbs.

We were living on the fourth floor, and it would not have been possible to run up and downstairs as often as was necessary for some. Therefore every room-unit soon did what all the others did: put up a bucket. Bourgeois modesty was soon pared down to the bare minimum, but this did not create healthier or more aesthetic relationships, only a growing revulsion and indifference toward others.

Eventually, horrible family scenes were enacted, in which the husband, contrary to normal behavior, exhibited a senile kind of weepiness while the wife spewed forth endless, shrill scolding that usually began with and culminated in the reproach that it was the husband's duty to provide for his family, but that he was somehow just lying around, pretending to be exhausted and letting his wife and children starve to death. And then the refrain: "You, being a man and therefore the strongest, should not shrink from any effort, any fight to prevent your family from going under."

Hunger

As I lie on dank floor boards,
Melting ice runs down the window pane.
Around me crowds of others lie,
They too are bathed in clammy sweat.

My belly is a watery balloon
On which wild Hunger drums a tune.
My innards ferment the loathsome swill
That backs up to my rising gorge.

My lungs are gasping, blubbering, wheezing,
And fever sucks my blood;
My spine is rattling, popping, crackling
As if tormented on a fiery grill.

And next to me lies someone else – you,
Fellow human, you, come closer!
I am not I, you are not you,
The two of us are bits of horrid flesh.

Hunger cuts into my gut
Like a fine sharp thread;
Purple swarms come rustling
Through my tormented brain.

I see my hands lie there before me,
Two swollen bits of green,
I see how cramps have bent my knees,
Pried wide by sudden chills.

The Self, the Me serves as the tool
That twists and bolts together limb and limb.
It turns and turns and never stops
Until it brings us to our fellow human's pain.

And next to me lies one in agony
Whose rattling groans come from a hollow depth,
And as he groans, his heavy tongue
Creeps from his gaping mouth.

You see, my fellow man, this is a tongue:
It is a helpless, naked animal,
It lumbers forward, ready to attack,
But all it can produce is drooling spit.

The tongue is fettered to the palate, a dog
Chained to a post;
Hunger is chained within the brain
And hammers it so hard that sparks are flying.

Hammers, and the crackling sparks
Plunge into meager residues of blood
And then go out. These little fires, everywhere,
Send burning smoke through all my crumbling bones.

Heeding imperious greetings from the sun,
The ice obeys and turns into a stream.
The water snakes around my naked feet
As if cajoling me with a moist kiss.

The wetness glues my ligaments together
And keeps my body in its slimy grip;
It has become a horrifying pastime
To listen to my groans as if they were not mine,

And also hear the groans of others as if they were my own.
Oh fellow-man, my lips are very white –
Soon I shall watch your eyes to see
How mine turn glassy ere they close forever.

But then it happened, almost at once: the men seemed to be getting taller and thinner. Their eyes sank into their heads, and their steps grew slower. And slowly, slowly the swellings began...

I was sick. All around me – beginning among the older members of the Frohmann family – cases of dysentery had been on the rise, and finally it was my turn. At that time I still had my mother, and she took care of me as only a mother can. Back and forth from the gas-kitchen she carried the heaviest pots, and she constantly climbed up and down three flights of stairs to empty the chamber pots. She washed my clothing in ice-cold water whenever it became necessary and shifted the blankets back and forth below me.

My healthy young body soon brought down the fever that had suddenly risen to 40° centigrade (104° Fahrenheit) and in about three days' time I was ready to get up.

One day Horst returned from work pale, tired, and excessively worn out. It was immediately clear to me that he had become infected, but he strenuously refused to even consider the thought of illness. I practically had to force him to take his temperature. It turned out that he had a fever of more than 104° Fahrenheit. My mother tried to look after him too as best she could, but he was oddly slow to recover.

In recent weeks we had had little time for each other. But now it was different. Both of us were ill, and suddenly we once again understood each other. Again and again I was seized by hot panic when I saw his increasingly emaciated body as he washed. His eyes were growing larger and larger, and his cheeks more and more pale and hollow.

Only once he said to me, "You can't imagine what I suffer at work. I should have learned to think around corners, but I haven't learned it so far, and I probably, alas, will never learn it. It is impossible for anyone able to think reasonably straight to eat the crap that other people are dishing up. I know that I'm going to croak, but I want you to believe how much I love you."

Covering his face with his hands, he groaned, "Why do I constantly have to think of my mother these days, of my sister and my dear little nephews. Why is that, oh why?" I heard this "why" from him many times thereafter, until at the end I made it my own.

Forced Labor

My numbed brow drops on the machine,
I fold my captive, tired hands.

A dangling yellow bulb sheds smoky light,
Dusk falls, the day grows pale.

The harried working hours are almost done,
The evening mist is waiting to embrace us.

What binds us in our common chains
Will only hold us while we work –
Night will find each of us in separate gloom.

Father continued to do his best to bring in vegetables and scanty quantities of any foodstuffs that might be available in his department. But the steady march of hunger could no longer be stopped.

Thereafter, perhaps in December, we had to move to a building in another part of the ghetto. On an ice-cold day we carried our few belongings on our backs through the crunchy snow and betook ourselves to a new abode. For Horst this move made life a little easier since his work place was on this side.

The ghetto was divided into two parts by a road that led from Lodz to one of its suburbs. For the Germans it would have been unthinkable to have Jews walk on this thoroughfare used also by members of the Master Race. They built three wooden bridges high above that narrow road. Indispensable wheeled traffic from the ghetto passed through several gates, guarded on one side by a German guard and on the other by a Jewish policeman. Getting around in the ghetto was made more difficult by these steep bridges and at times of heavy snow falls or icy conditions, one had to stand in line for hours before crossing over.

Constantly teeming with people who dragged their water-logged feet in one direction or the other, the bridges became the defining feature of the ghetto.

We came to a tall, ramshackle house with narrow stone stairs, a drafty place. The twenty-two persons in our dwelling unit, having become accustomed to each other's ways, did not want to separate again. On the fourth floor we found a room with an adjoining kitchen. The kitchen had a broken-down stove, a window half of which had fallen out, damp walls and floors. The adjoining room was in no better shape.

Our family made do with the kitchen. The powers that be felt that four persons were not entitled to an entire kitchen and added two persons, a gentleman and a lady, brother and sister who wordlessly joined us. They placed their suitcases in a corner, sat down on them, and stared at each other in silence. He, tall and well-built, looked like someone in his mid-thirties,

although he actually was in his fifties. He had a fair-skinned, broad, well-cut face. His sister was smaller, too thin. Out of an ample fur coat peered a timid, homely face that lacked youth but had kind dark eyes under a shock of dark hair styled in a masculine cut.

He stared into a corner for at least fifteen minutes, then paced back and forth in great agitation, and finally sat down again without uttering a word. To us who had learned not to make a fuss and to deal with the givens in an unemotional and sober manner that focused on the necessities of the moment, his behavior seemed excessive and disagreeable. For the time being we made no attempt to communicate with them at all.

My mother went to work on the broken stove trying all kinds of tricks to fix it well enough to provide a bit of heat for us. To a limited extent she succeeded.

We knew that as the weather turned colder it would become difficult for most people to continue their daily habit of going to the gas-kitchen on the other side of the bridge. We decided to do our best to give everyone the opportunity to cook on our stove or to warm themselves. For a small sum that everyone had to contribute, we were able to buy enough coal to keep the heat going.

The heat produced by the ramshackle stove was minimal. We were glad that we did not have to spend all day like most of the others, lying around on the floor huddled in our blankets.

Efforts were under way to give a new name to the form of our communal life. We became a "Collective." The only change was that the communal kitchen was taken over by our own people, and that the opportunity for stealing changed over from the Polish Jews to us. The intent had been to integrate resettled newcomers into the normal housing system of the ghetto and to provide them with the individual food rations to which they were entitled. This would have been a major improvement for many people. Also, a decrease in the number of people assigned to a single room would have reduced the danger of epidemics.

All of us would have been spared the revolting manifestations of envy arising from the various gradations of being hungry, as well as the constant shrill screaming about thefts that had occurred. Now the camp's leadership, in league with the many ideological jerks infatuated with "socialism and community," raised their voices. For two days the house was filled with the sound of quarreling factions.

I felt a strange pulling at my heart strings when I saw the edema-ridden people in the stairways, in their rooms, in other places, stinking with dysentery, staring straight ahead in their hunger, and creeping about moaning softly to themselves. Those who still had the strength to yell, yelled. The poisoned tools of misery had drilled right into the abysses of human nature, and what welled up was the chaos of futility.

And so the outcome was: A Collective! As always, the better-fed won. They were the keepers of Life, Civilization, Culture, Ethics, Love, and Charity. The hungry were allowed to keep their right to perplexity and – malice of fate – their fear of death. All the group transports became Collectives. In this manner the division between the long established Jews in the ghetto and the newcomers was made final. We no longer received food coupons and thus remained dependent on the daily issues of watery, fatless, and inedible soups.

I soon became so weak that I was barely able to leave my blanket. I was fully aware of the dangers of giving in. I began to write and had ample opportunity to speak to my neighbors, the brother and sister pair. He was a radio dramaturge from Vienna. Both of them made much of the fact that they were born in Austria and not in Germany. This appeared to be a congenital disease of most Austrians, making their stupidity even more conspicuous.

Only, Fritz was not stupid. He was blasé in a pathetic sort of way. His bald pate, embedded in a wreath of hair, looked like a monkish tonsure, a look that he was almost able to carry off by dint of his dramatic meekness. He was as melancholy as any old woman and as venomous and inexhaustible in his vituperations as the fools of both sexes. However, he was possessed of an attractive measure of genuine cultivation.

I got along well with him, although we sometimes swapped terrible insults. His sister was a good-natured little goose, who idolized and admired her Fritz. Out of a certain emotional infantilism born of hunger, I became extraordinarily fond of her. These were people with whom I could talk, and that was necessary.

Horst's condition became more and more serious. He was in a state of excessive fatigue whenever he returned from work, but he did not follow my advice to take a rest. In constant fear of my parents' contempt, he never wanted to show any weakness.

I saw that his eyes kept sinking deeper and deeper into their orbits and often looked dull and apathetic from sheer weakness and distress. And Lord, I also knew what he had to suffer at work. He no longer wanted to acknowledge this, but I could feel it. He was caught in a clash of two worlds, which could not coexist, and which were bound to devour each other. And then the weaker would provide nourishment for the stronger.

Horst, weakened by hunger and emotional suffering, was unable to continue the fight. More than once I felt that the threat of his sacrifice was drawing closer. He lost weight. The flesh gradually melted off his body. Bones protruded from all sides, and after a time the flames of fever began to flicker around his limbs and to scorch him.

I begged and pleaded with him to stop going to work, but he would not hear of it until one day they brought him home to me. I felt shame at the sight of the emaciated faces with the burning eyes, their gaunt bodies wrapped in rags, when they laid him down before me. They silently warmed their stiffened hands by the embers without a word of sympathy or comfort, slaves of hunger and also its priests. I understood these men and respected their aloofness. I knew about the yawning chasm between them and us and felt an immense heaviness.

On that day again I was unable to think, a prey to vertigo. Horst had gone to see the doctor, who had ordered a saliva test for his T.B. I kept praying, obstinately and without thinking: "Not positive, please not positive! Look, he is still so young, and it has been so wonderful. Why should it be over already, over forever. Please! Please, this once. Not yet positive!" I sensed that the All-Powerful-One was smiling, and I fell silent.

The next morning, a rumpled heap of gray blankets lay on the floor. A bony skull prickly with black stubble stuck out of it. High cheek bones under a skin burning with fever. Thin and bluish lids that covered the protruding orbs of the irises.

Outside the ground turned to sticky clay. The sky crept away, the earth crept away. Only Misery stood its ground, big and pallid. The almighty specter of That-Which-Will-Always-Be filled the narrow streets. They pull the excrement wagon. "Gee up, whoa, gee up!" Ten slaves they are, covered with filth, staggering from sheer deprivation, shod in wooden clogs that weigh down their feet filled with the edema of hunger. "Gee up, whoa, gee up!" Ten loads they must cart by noon, else there will be no soup. "Gee up, whoa!" The hot soup, the red soup, the eternal soup. "Gee up, whoa!" I am cold. I am terribly cold. I tremble all over. A slight nausea grips my throat. A groan from Horst. "Please get up, I have to shake out the blankets."

The Blankets

I shake out the blankets, the sad, sad blankets,
Filled with misery, dust, and pain,
And bury beneath them my longing, a searing longing
For sensuous pleasure and warmth.

I caress the mirror, the time-stained mirror,
And as I cover its cracked old face
My lips, starved and blue,
Kiss the memory of eyes once reflected there.

I smooth out my hair, my dry, straggly hair,
As if to smooth out my poor heart's confusion.
Alas, between torn shirt and ribs
Longing is covered with dust.

A small bowl of water – it just licks my hands
And misery freezes my pulse.
I shake out the blankets, the sad, sad blankets,
And bury beneath them my longing for warmth.

The snow was slowly vanishing from the window. Melting ice was dripping, and a light-gray sun inched its way through the filmy windows. The brother and sister were still lying down, he staring over to us with expressive pity, she shivering with cold and weeping softly. I too was shivering. Horst lay motionless.

Izrael Lejzerowicz,
Sewage Cart in the Lodz Ghetto

Crayon on paper, 43.5 x 67.2 cm.
Gift of Nachman Zonabend, Sweden.

(Courtesy of the Yad Vashem Art Museum, Jerusalem)

The dramaturge brother had found this scrap of paper with my poem somewhere and read it aloud in a mocking tone. I was so angry that I felt like hitting him. Horst just peered at me with a sad smile. I asked him not to get up any more. Something within me screamed, "Why have You just chucked him down there, a helpless little pile of perishing life? Why do You let him die like a dog, when he never learned to act like a dog, and why do You allow all the sleek dogs with their shiny pelts to feed on his carcass? For shame! Away from me, away from me, I detest Your justice!" And then again, "Not positive, please, please, not positive."

"What did the doctor tell you?" Through clenched teeth he whispered, "Perhaps you should go to see the doctor yourself, talk to him. He didn't want to tell me anything; the results were not in yet." His trembling and anxious voice moved me deeply and yet made me angry, for I was constantly shaken by flashes of rebellion against seeing this brittle life crumble in my hands.

Much too eagerly I grabbed my coat: "I'm going, going right away." Making my way through the mud, I slowly pulled my feet out of one lump of sticky clay only to have them sink into the next one. Again a thin rain dribbled out of the heavy low clouds. Mixed with blowing snow it pelted my face, stung my eyes, and further chilled my empty stomach where water was sloshing.

I have to cross the bridge. Masses of people heavily roll over it, black and panting, they slowly move. The bridge sways softly. Its steps make a loud grating noise, but it holds. Rigidly rising in its unconcern, it sways and it grates. People stand in line stoically waiting on either side of the bridge. Policemen stand there, stomping their feet. They are on duty, but it looks as if they too were waiting.

In the doctor's waiting room there is another long line of people. They stomp their feet, rail, shove, and rail again. Rumors are flitting back and forth among them, the eternally renewed, eternally ridiculed, and eternally believed rumors that liberation is near. It is the eternal and irresistible emanation of the survival instinct.

Men and women walk by in shiny, well-polished boots and solid overcoats, wearing the silky marks of shame and humiliation on their well-padded chests and backs.

Silky, beautifully stitched badges of shame they are – a sign, it seems to me, that people love to adorn themselves with golden chains. If they find a way to make their misery look pretty, they think they have overcome it.

The doctor's office was bare. Several wooden benches stood along the walls. Some men were undressing. They had become emaciated skeletons with burning, prominent cheekbones. They were like all the men of the ghetto who had no opportunity to steal food. They were like Horst and also, now, my father.

The doctor sat behind a wide wooden table, bald and beady-eyed. In front of him lay his red-rimmed cap with the Aesculapius staff. He examined his patients slowly, and then casually mumbled something that I could not understand. Even though he spoke German, he was a resettled person himself.

The snake seemed about to uncoil itself from the staff. I stared at it as if hypnotized and suddenly had to pull myself together, for he had addressed me. "What can I do for you? Oh yes, you are the fiancée of poor Horst Appel. Please, have a seat." He suddenly became very friendly, and I was frightened, as frightened as never before in my life. I choked on my words.

He looked at me for a long time trying to decide if I could take it. Then he pushed a small white piece of paper across the table: "Koch plus. Billions present in the field of vision." Not only all thinking, all feeling too now drained from me. I stared at him uncomprehendingly. Then he started speaking, softly, between clenched teeth, "You are pretty good-looking, I am surprised that you are able to cope, now that your sweetheart is awaiting death."

I continued to stare uncomprehendingly at his bared teeth and felt the snake slithering toward me from its staff. The whole square, bare room seemed to revolve around me in a wild whirl, and for the first time ever I felt a violent desire to kill. But nothing happened. The doctor continued to smile his forced smile, and I was gripped by a spasm of emotion that forced me to my knees. "It cannot be," I sobbed, "no, it cannot be!" He stroked my hair and said in a revoltingly melancholy tone, "Child, child, you are still so young. Perhaps you'll survive. But we old folks, well, it's up to God!"

"Thank you very much, Doctor, thank you!" I negligently stuffed some of the papers he had handed me into my pocket and was soon outside. The rain, mixed with snow, dripped down inexorably.

They had an infirmary which did absolutely nothing to help, but Horst was put into quarantine, and I couldn't have any contact with him at all. I wrote him a letter every day, and he wrote me a letter every day until he died. My mother and I went hunting for dandelions. We were from the country, and we knew our way around. We went to the cemetery. Dandelions were growing there, and we gathered them. We used the greens to supplement our food, and we took them to him at the the infirmary every day. I prevailed upon my parents and myself to give part of our rations to my boyfriend, and my mother was willing to do it. I don't know why she did that. She did it. We all did it. I had no right to do that.

No injustice should be permitted to happen to the companion of my earliest youth and of my first great misery and distress. He died – and thus – so I will it –may he live on…

From that last day on I fought a running battle against the survival instinct of a lot of hungry young women, namely, the officials sitting behind desks in the dark corridors of the ghetto's hospitals. They were not polite – and this has gone down as funny in the lore of these young ladies – no indeed, for they were hungry, as hungry as you and I, and they understood us only too well. They were not compassionate – God forbid! – not compassionate at all. Our yellow stars and theirs looked so damned alike.

It was clear to me: there will be no mercy here. Here only one thing counted: protection! So many – oh so terribly many – stood in line, and each one of them carried the same burden of misery as the next person. To step out of that line, one had to grasp the proverbial "little finger" held out by fate. How odd that all of us, every last one, kept looking for that little finger, which always seemed to dangle somewhere from an indifferent sky.

Few, very few, see it, and even fewer are able to grab it. And always only one attaches oneself like a nursling to the breast, sucking in conceited familiarity as if to devour the whole hand.

Horst Appel, 1918-1942

The Mass Grave at Marysin

A square room, dank and cold,
And on the floor a writhing blanket,
Black stubble on a withered skull
With heavy bags around the sunken eyes.

Convulsively two hands jab through the air,
A gurgling stammer issues from the chest:
"Not far from here, in Marysin,
A grave is waiting for my miserable bones!"

My throat chokes on my words; about to slump
I feel snow blowing in through every gap.
Summoning Death with my last strength,
I stare expectantly – yet never fall.

He writhes, and I hear the hideous sound
Of bone on bone. Twenty-one years,
Twenty-one years old. The fever's flames
Have left a little pile of ashes on the bier.

The snow comes thicker now through all the gaps.
Where once my heart was is a deep black cavern
Filled to the brim with blood and tears, with dirt, dried
Mud, and also other filth that I have spawned myself.

We loved each other once, oh how we loved!
The croaking of the crows comes through the broken panes.
Left is a fever-eaten skull, black stubble, and the groaning
From my breast that will not go away.

"Not far from here, in Marysin, a grave awaits!"
There will your bones give cover to my shame. Swirling
Snow, white and endless, fills the air –
And icy cold undoes the pain-racked bonds.

Lejzerowicz

Upstairs from the quarters in which we dwelled lived a painter, Lejzerowicz by name. To my seventeen-year-old romantic mind, he represented the example of a nineteenth-century artist. I made friends with him, told him of my interest in poetry, and he invited me to attend literary gatherings held in his room.

One of the physiological results of constant hunger and near starvation is the total preoccupation with food, so that one is unable to think or talk of anything else, and even one's dreams at night are filled with visions of food. These get-togethers became a beacon in the relentless darkness and a reminder that my existence need not be solely focused upon food and survival from hour to hour, day by day, but that there were, indeed, other dimensions.

The language of the ghetto was full of expressions to give voice to its inexpressible horrors but also making use of the gallows humor so often connected to the Jewish experience in history.

Lejzerowicz led a charmed existence in the ghetto, protected by the president whose portraits he painted and through whose connection he was even to paint portraits of Gestapo officials who provided paints and canvas. Having connections, which was called Protekcja, *was of extreme importance. Nothing was as important as one's connections in the ghetto. Through Lejzerowicz, I got some connections. He was able to get me a job, and I insisted that he also get my mother a job in the factory where we then got extra food.*

Izrael Lejzerowicz lived with his father in a room in Rybna 14A. It was a flight of stairs up from the kitchen which my parents and I occupied.

His hair was quite long, his face pale and sickly, but his eyes were brightly alive. His nose was long and aquiline between high cheekbones, and the mouth seemed to move even when he was not speaking. He had the long slender hands of the artist and the hunchback, both of which he was.

*Painter/Poet Izrael Lejzerowicz
by one of the bridges
that separated two sections
of the Lodz ghetto*

*(photograph by Mendel Grossman,
courtesy Ghetto Fighters' House, Israel)*

The room upstairs served as their living quarters and the studio for him. As I got to know him, he invited me to his room. His father seemed to be permanently seated in a large wooden armchair in a corner of the room so as to make up part of the furnishings. He bore no resemblance to his son whatsoever. I remember him wearing a Polish cap and a long, patriarchal beard, a silent man. His bed filled one alcove and a spittoon stood right next to it.

Lejzerowicz coughed a lot, and he complained of a heart condition. He said that at night he could hear himself galloping away upon the beat of his heart. He also told me of his recurring dreams of running breathlessly through unending libraries, knowing that the books he passed would never be read.

There were paintings leaning against the wall, stacked in all the corners and half finished on two easels. His paintings were mostly of the Lodz ghetto which enveloped us, of the huge wooden bridges which connected the parts of the ghetto and which spanned the roads of the Gentile city.

As regards the cultural club that Lejzerowicz had assembled, these were eight to ten men and women of the ghetto who all needed to express the bewilderment and horror they were living. All but myself were Polish Jews, most likely natives of Lodz. Most came from a Yiddishist culture, although I remember one young man who was writing in Polish. Lejzerowicz wrote in both languages. We were all enthusiastically critiquing each other, even though my understanding of the others' contributions was, at best, imperfect, as, I would imagine, my German was to them. The experience of the literary circle lasted for a year or two.

I learned Yiddish in the ghetto, in Lodz. I had not really heard it until then. Even the children of people born in Eastern Europe who had emigrated to Germany didn't know much Yiddish. Many of them had attended the seminary. They understood Yiddish because their parents spoke it. Children of those who were born in Germany never learned Yiddish. There was never any call for it. I can understand it if I ask people to speak slowly – not everything, because there are so many words mixed in that are not of German origin.

The ghetto was run by the Germans, and for me, a Jew, to be speaking German was to be, by far, in the minority.

How enmeshed in language we all are. Yiddish, Polish, German, the language of the enemy, the torturer, the red-clawed beast waiting outside the ghetto! I was speaking its language, even celebrating it in poetry, in my urge to give voice to my feelings. It was the only tool in my possession, and it was befouled.

It didn't really matter whether or not I understood every word of the others' writing. Their laments had to be more authentic. They were written in a Jewish language, which even made use of the Hebrew alphabet. Lejzerowicz read his verses in a hollow, softly fluting voice, which I thought quite enchanting. There was another young girl who wrote in Polish, who was much acclaimed by the others. She had remarkably large eyes and Lejzerowicz once noted that she had the looks of a true poetess, which caused me pangs of jealousy.

It is hard to say how much of my writing was, indeed, understood by my friends. Much is made of the German extraction of Yiddish. Over the centuries Yiddish has taken on linguistic characteristics of its own which parody its progenitor, German, while it removes its romanticism, adds irony and a Hebraic exotic flavor totally lacking from the original. No wonder that it has been looked down upon as the deformed, despised stepchild. But I learned in the ghetto in Lejzerowicz's room, around the rickety wooden table, that this poor, uncouth foundling had learned to use the tongue passionately and honestly. Yiddish was made for crying, but also for screaming and cursing. It was the perfect language for the ghetto.

Nevertheless, my friends were kind to me. They listened to my German words with sympathy and interest, claimed they understood it all perfectly, and encouraged me to continue since we would all meet again "in freedom" to continue our literary diversion, to benefit the remnant of the Jewish people, and to light the outer darkness of the rest of mankind.

This Is My Tongue

This is my tongue, nailed
To a language that curses me:
It was hammered
Into my ears
With the tones of love
And of consuming hate.

These are reflections kept within my soul:
The mighty specters of undying books,
The ancient spires of hometowns,
Verdant beech groves, small hurrying streams,
And the stars that stand above them at night.

These are reflections that came through my eyes:
The printed filth of screeching pamphlets,
The walls of barbed wire,
The well-cemented dungeons of shame,
And the searchlights that spew poison into the dusk.

Love and hate have carried me
To this cross to which my heart is welded,
And my tongue too.

Genagelt ist meine Zunge

Genagelt ist meine Zunge
an eine Sprache, die mich verflucht,
hineingehämmert
in meine Ohren
mit den Tönen der Liebe,
und des fressenden Hasses.

Hineingespiegelt
in meine Seele
die mächtigen Geister ewiger Schriften,
die alten Türme der Städte,
die grünenden Buchenwälder,
die Flüsse kleine und eilige
und die Sterne, die nächtens darüberstehen.

Hereingespiegelt
in meine Augen
der gedruckte Unrat keifender Pamphlete,
der sperrende Stacheldraht,
die wohlgemauerten Verließe der Schande,
und die Scheinwerfer, die das Gift in die Dämmerung jagen.

Liebe und Hass haben sich getragen
zum Kreuz, an das mein Herz geschmiedet ist
und meine Zunge.

I Travel Back

I travel back to the border of life
Wrapped in my bristly pain,
A tariff is owed on the hate I carry – but never mind,
Life itself is hatred, is brimming with hate.

Just behind me smoke still rises from deadly stones,
Just behind me madness and horror still reign.
But then death is death, and life is life –
I shake the sand from my wooden clogs.

The inspector inspects me with narrowed eyes,
And then cancels my bill, and cancels my burden,
And cancels the shortfall, the debt I racked up
In riotous dealings with death.

I unfurl my pain round my bony limbs,
Hurl hatred and sand into the chimney,
And sit down by the entrance in deep despair –
Alive, but a beggar, a beggar.

A Child No More

My grandparents were very quickly separated from us into an old people's home, which the Ghetto-Chief had set up in order to provide better housing for the old and the weak among the resettled population. When I visited them for the first time, I was rather pleased with the improvement of their situation. At least they were given cots with straw-filled mattresses. They slept in rooms that were cleaned every day, and, at first, the food was clean and somewhat more generous than ours.

I went there many times. Once my grandmother told me that she thought she had lice. It was a terrible thing, but in Lodz it was so common. Somebody gave me a lice comb, and I sat there combing my grandmother's hair, and I felt so humiliated. She was such an immaculate lady.

It's a custom among German Jews, after you have been married for a year, that somebody in the family gives you tachrichim. Tachrichim means the clothes that you get buried in, a white shroud. It's a very sobering thing, but I guess it's supposed to keep you on the straight and narrow. The custom among German Jews was that they sew their own tachrichim. And so my grandmother took her tachrichim and my grandfather's tachrichim with her to the ghetto, and they were buried in them. They died within six months because later on they didn't feed them anything. They were willing to eliminate the old people first. Fortunately, they didn't get loaded on a truck to be taken to the gas chambers.

The time of fairy tales has long since passed,
The time of golden wings;
Enclosed within the garden, deep in thought, I am
A horse in iron reins.

I rear, I scream –
I scream to scatter
The new and horrifying tale.
I am child no more …

There's a subtle change that took place from being a child, listening to your parents, and then there's a switch of authority. I was young, but I was healthier, and I was less hopeless, perhaps because I still had that life force in me, being young. When you're an adult and you see what's going on, there wasn't much to hope for. It's just the fact that you're young, you feel invulnerable. Children always feel invulnerable. They do crazy things, and that is the advantage of being young. If you can preserve that in a situation like in the ghetto, it gives you a kind of authority.

So the role was reversed, and that seemed to be commonplace. I started to take on the responsibility for my parents. My mother was forty. I looked at her. I knew that she was older. I had to take responsibility. My father was eleven years older than my mother. He was quite capable, but they just let me do whatever I wanted to. If I made a decision, I made a decision.

The World Was Once So Big and Wide

Our house was located right next to the barbed wire fence that barred us from the outside world. Every day I silently communed with the nearby and yet so terribly faraway freedom. The guard stood almost directly under our window. In the course of one such moment of contemplation, the following poem came to me:

The world was once so big and wide,
Now it has shrunk to a ghetto's size,
From fence to wire fence.

Clouds, stop roaming across the sky,
How dare you float
So freely over this fence.

The guard stands in his sentry-box
Peering from side to side,
He clutches his gun to his heart.

He must make sure that not one little puddle
Runs to the other side,
Remember, we shoot to kill.

White ground here, white ground there:
Surely now, God in his wisdom
Is keeping the races apart.

Here it's called *Schnai*, over there no doubt *Schnee*.
The guard, staring dully ahead,
Ponders this difference in words.

The storm howls and whistles around the house.
Tell us, Storm, of the outside world,
Tell us how all this will end.

The guard in dangerous calm
Just watches the raging storm,
Holding the gun in his hands.

I had another idea. I went to the manager of the factory who was a Polish-speaking, assimilated Jew, still well dressed, but I knew he was hungry. So was everybody else in the ghetto. There was a small field in front of the factory, and I said, "You know my father is a farmer. If you can get him some seed potatoes, he can plant potatoes. He can plant any place. He's very good at that. And then if you share it with us, we'll both have potatoes." He said, "Okay." He got seed potatoes, my father planted them, and we had potatoes, a sack of potatoes one winter. He got one half, and we got the other half. So that's really how we lived in the ghetto. We had to look for ways to survive.

One lived from day to day, the whole time, almost four years. One had no sense of tomorrow. If you had a meal today, you lived today. You couldn't really plan for tomorrow. I had no idea what the time of month was. I had no calendar, no newspaper, and no idea. It was timeless, like we lived on an island all by ourselves. There's no other world. It was like it was an island under siege, and the enemy was right in front of the door and could come in any time. You just had to survive another day.

Every morning the grave-diggers would come around. People had put the dead, the corpses, outside, and they would load up the corpses, and they would take them to the cemetery. They had to bury them too. They had to dig the graves. It was very, very difficult, very hard for them. In the beginning, they had horses to drive these wagons, but then the horses were eaten, and the wagons were pulled by people. There were more and more cadaverous people. They could hardly move. Four or five of them would pull this wagon. These were the circumstances in which we lived for several years.

E arly in 1944 my mother got sick. My parents were healthy strong people so they lasted that long. People got all kinds of diseases from the lice. Lice carry diseases. Washing was a big problem. Many times we would go outside and wash. There were no bathrooms there. There were latrines outside, and we would go outside and wash ourselves in the snow. My mother would stand in front of me and put some cover in front of me. I would stand behind it and rub myself in snow. Then I would hold it for her, and she would do the same.

In early 1944, it was cold, and she was burning with fever. At night I lay next to her, listening to her rapid breathing. She had curly hair in braids, and it was in my face, and I felt the heat from her body. I really did not want my mother to die. I started to pray again. I had become wise to the ways of death in the ghetto, and I knew there was no help for us from human sources. I had prayed often in the ghetto, but never more intensely than now.

I walked through the muddy streets of Lodz with tears rolling down my face wondering whether I would have the courage to offer my own life instead of hers and whether that would matter at all. I said, "You have to do this for me. You have to do this for me. That's all I ask of You. Let her live. Let her live." Really, I was having a fight with God. I said, "I'm not promising to be good; I'm not promising anything. I'm not making any bargains. Why should You do this to me? She's a wonderful woman."

I recounted her great virtues. "She took care of her sister-in-law who was retarded, and she took care of my father's parents, and she was just a young girl. How hard she worked, and she didn't deserve this. Let her live!" I remember all these things going through my mind. I really prayed to God to save her, but at the same time I knew it couldn't be done, that I wouldn't have the power to save her. I didn't win, and she died. That was one of the most painful times.

They finally took her to the infirmary. My friend who arranged that said, "Why shouldn't she be comfortable and lie in a real bed?" and I agreed. They shaved her hair off. I said, "I shouldn't have let her go." When I visited, I could see the growing isolation from life in her eyes, both wide open but gazing from life into the imminent darkness. During all my years under the various forms

Before My Mother's Death

This is the last time, Mother dearest,
That you opened your eyes to me;
Out of these eyes, Mother dearest,
Death looks at me with a leer.

Your mouth has grown silent, Mother dearest,
But the light of your eyes speaks to me,
Farewell, I will never be mother
Nor you the child again.

The glance of your eyes, Mother dearest,
Follows me as I reach for the door,
And then from your eyes, oh Mother,
My life is gone – and yours.

Vor dem Tode meiner Mutter

Du hast die Augen, liebe Mutter,
zum letzten Mal mir aufgetan,
aus diesen Augen, liebe Mutter,
sieht mich der Tod schon grinsend an.

Starr ist dein Mund schon, liebe Mutter,
so sagen deiner Augen Schein,
Leb wohl, ich werde niemals Mutter
und nie wirst du mein Kind mehr sein.

Mit deinen Augen, liebe Mutter,
folgst du mir lang zur Tür hinaus,
dann löscht in deinen Augen, Mutter,
mein Leben aus – dein Leben aus.

of oppression and threats of annihilation, I had always been able to maintain a sense of detachment, as if the horror around me was somehow not touching me directly. That I was able to observe and record is evidenced by the poems I wrote in which I was able to sublimate my fears.

She didn't look at me. She looked straight up. I looked in her eyes, and I just knew she saw me. She knew I was there. I held her hand, and then I helped her to go on the pot, the same thing with my grandmother too. As the last minute came she said, "Child, help me," and then I helped her get to the pot. She had diarrhea, and she fell back into bed, and I stood there, and she never said anything to me. I wanted her to say something. She didn't say anything.

My mother was only forty-one years old when she died, a healthy, vigorous woman, who had labored hard all her life serving her demanding extended family and all who had contact with her. What I mourned mostly was her selflessness, even self-negation. Where was her reward? May her memory be for a blessing!

The cart took her to Marysin. My father and I stood at her graveside. My father gave a eulogy of sorts: "She was a wonderful wife for me." I felt angry. I thought, that's not all she was, just a wife to you. My mother was a wonderful woman who did the best she could in her life, which was short. I guess he just wasn't full of high-flying words at that time.

Rumkowski, Eldest of the Jews, was ordered to liquidate the ghetto. He had to provide a certain number of people every once in a while to be eliminated. That's when all this fiction of the work transports came about. People volunteered and were segregated in a special place in the ghetto until they had enough together and would ship them out.

There was also such a thing as a selection in the ghetto. In every picture one sees of Lodz, one sees these huge wooden bridges that the Germans built across the city streets so the Jews wouldn't come into contact with the Poles. Whenever the Germans came in to make a selection, they closed off the bridges so they segregated everybody in little pockets and would order everybody out of the houses. Then they would go in and stick their bayonets into the ceiling and shoot into the ceilings to flush people out. They lined people up in the courtyards and in the streets and picked up all the older people and children. They had big trucks with a big red cross painted on them. They said they were going to a place where life would be easier. Of course, there was no such thing as the Red Cross. People were taken to Chelmno and eliminated.

Then my father got sick. He caught it, and I didn't. After my mother died, I had a severe cold, and I was spitting blood. I was sure that I had caught it. I was right next to her. It's amazing what your mind can do. It can make you sick; it can make you well. I willed myself not to have it. I can't even say I was really fighting it. I felt it would only be right if I got it.

The word was out in the ghetto that volunteers were sought for resettlement into another camp. Most of us did not comprehend the implication of this resettlement.

I didn't want my father to die in the ghetto. Nothing could be worse than the ghetto. I didn't yet know about those ovens. I volunteered my father and myself. My father did not object. We were taken to a separate enclave within the ghetto, waiting for sufficient "volunteers" to fill the quota.

Rumkowski came into this enclave, which was barred to anyone from entering or leaving. He was riding in his lordly droschke, a horse-drawn carriage. This was his transportation in the ghetto. With him was my friend, the painter. Lejzerowicz presented me to the president with high praises for my literary ability. He pointed out that, if helped to survive, I would want to record the merits of Mr. Rumkowski, the sacrifices he had made, and the brilliant leadership he had provided for the ghetto of Lodz. He believed it. Everything flattering he believed.

Rumkowski said, "Your father is sick. We will take him to the hospital." I figured that he would lie in a bed, and it would be clean. They had doctors, some of the best doctors from Czechoslovakia, who starved with everybody else, but they had clean clothes.

I remained silent and was, therefore, saved from what would have been certain death. My father and I were returned to the ghetto and the misery that we were familiar with. They took him to the hospital in the horse-drawn carriage. My father was a farmer down to his core. He was sitting behind the driver with me. He loved it, sitting behind a horse, just wonderful. So he had some moments there that I treasure. They are like jewels, these memories of my father.

They had a large room in the hospital and some resources. I put on the best dress I had and went to see my father. I whistled to him, and he was so happy to see me. He said to the man in the next bed, "That's my daughter. I have another one. Well, who knows?" I could just see the pride in his eyes and that alone was worth it. I was happy that I could do that. I visited as much as I could, until they wouldn't let me in. At least he died in a bed, and I was the one, the only one, who went to the cemetery with him. After that, I realized I wasn't ever going to be a child again. I was on my own.

Lejzerowicz told me, "You know that the Eldest has an orphanage?" I said, "Never heard of it. He has an orphanage?" I knew he had been the head of an orphanage before. He said, "No, no, he has a place here in Lodz, where he has some kids that he picked out, and they live much better. They have more food, and I'll get you into it."

I had a much better life in the orphanage. I was nineteen. I was older than most of them. I was older by a couple of years, but Rumkowski took me in. I had one unpleasant experience. He liked young girls it turned out, much younger girls. He actually liked little girls. He had all kinds of kinks in his nature. He felt me up and down. I didn't know that was coming. I didn't know what to do. I didn't want to run away because here my life was at stake. But nothing like that had ever happened before. The place was really quite nice, and I got more food for about four weeks before we were all transported to Auschwitz.

Within a few weeks, they emptied the ghetto. I had heard that the Russians had come very close. I thought they were going to come in and liberate us, but that wasn't happening. The Germans, in their love for the Jews, wanted to take us with them, and they did. They emptied out the whole ghetto, one transport after another. I found out later that all but two of these went to Auschwitz. Two transports carrying top ghetto officials and their families reportedly went to work camps in Germany.

The Train

Hurtling through the night – a sultry cavern
That has devoured our happy land –
A train roars over moist and shiny tracks,
Clattering, crashing toward unknown blackness.

Moonlight here and there leaks through the clouds,
A frightened little star peers down.
Rivers gurgle at this slight disturbance
But soon fall silent, wrapped into the night.

Deep in a forest of ten thousand trees
A breeze springs up and flies to bring relief,
But nowhere can it seep through wired windows:
The railroad cars are tightly sealed.

The night is sultry, moist and musty. The cars
Are filled with stifling heat that does not move.
Soft moans are heard from wizened, white-haired grandmas
And the thin voices of the little ones.

Bags, much too heavy, press from every side,
Sticking to the moist and sweaty bodies
Of those who gasp from throats gone dry with fear
And bore their eyes into impenetrable dark.

"Mother, I cannot breathe!" – No answer.
"Mother, I cannot breathe!" – barely a sigh.
Wedged among the bags – oh, much too heavy –
Sits the mother, feeling deep within her
Something swelling, writhing in despair.

And still she tries and tries: "God, just give me hope!"
Yet as she speaks the train lets out a terrifying shriek,
Wildly leaps backward, and then,
Its frenzied pace renewed, plunges ahead once more.

The backward lurch has loosened all the bags
And tossed them right into the people's space,
But then the forward jolt throws back the lot,
Bag and baggage, kith and kin.

Onward speeds the train – darkness recedes.
Confused, the clouds rush back and forth
From daylight here to darkness there,
Until the dawn spreads everywhere.

Suddenly, like a gaping maw,
A soaring arch looms ahead,
With shiny grasping teeth of pointed guns,
And greedy tongues of blood-red flags.

In blind haste the train rushes through it –
The day not fully dawned.
Twilight covers this vast grey earth,
And the sun cowers behind the clouds.

"Halt!" – A sharp jolt, no more motion.
The whole train has been swallowed up.
Inside the silence grows heavy –
Shadows watch through the windows and doors.

Shadows open the windows and doors,
Shiny skulls project into the cars
their sneering grins.
These are the bowling balls that death will throw.

But no, you are received by human beings;
They're made of blood and bones, nay, even flesh.
Obedient to their ancient master, Terror,
They earnestly, in silence, do their work.

Among the yapping dogs green devils loiter,
Puffing on cigarettes.
Expectantly they slap their little leather whips
Against their boots.

Children tumble, wizened grandmas,
Men and women; like a hideous cloud-burst,
Human beings, human beings
Are pouring from the railroad cars.

Ever tighter do the bony fingers
Of Terror grip the long-constricted throats;
No panting breaks the awful silence,
But here and there the whips are hissing.

The sun has not yet mustered
The force of its sharp light,
Floating in a reddish hue behind gray clouds
It sways in a blur.

Between barbed wires and the barracks
The well-paved road runs on:
Never yet has a boot slipped here
On a puddle of blood or tears.

To the right waits a gate, to the left a chimney –
And a jerk of the thumb points the way.
Here and there a small squeaky voice: "Mother, Mother!"
And then there is fire and the sun comes up.

Auschwitz

*M*y sister had already been in Auschwitz for a year or so when she heard that transports from Lodz were coming. She knew our parents and I were there. When she was in Berlin she got a card from my parents saying, "We have been resettled to the East." She heard from other people that it could be Lodz or, as the Germans called it, Litzmannstadt. There were quite a few transports coming from Lodz, and she kept asking people if they knew us. Finally she took it upon herself – it took a tremendous amount of courage – to march up to the Obersturmführer, the camp commander of Auschwitz. She said, respectfully, "Heil Obersturmführer, Heil Kommandant, *number 37468 makes herself known.*"

He looked at her and said, "Who are you?" She said, "My name is Carol Stern," and he looked at her. "How long have you been here?" She told him, "two years." He said, "What do you want, Häftling (prisoner)?" She said, "May I approach the commandant?" He said, "Yeah, come here." She said, "I know that there are lots of transports coming from Lodz, from the ghetto. I have my sister and my parents there. Would it be okay if I were to go to the ramp with you when you make a selection? Can I bring my parents and my sister here?" He said to her, "You speak German fluently. Where are you from?" She figured he wouldn't know our small village, or would maybe think it was in Poland, so she said "Frankfurt." He said, "Oh, okay." Then he said, "You can't go, but if you know some male person, I'll take him to the ramp and we'll try."

Then he noticed that my sister was wearing a ring. She had found it on the campgrounds. He said, "Where did you get that?" She said, "I don't even know who gave me the ring." He said, "What is that engraving? You should have it engraved on your skin." He suddenly became sorry he showed a human emotion so he immediately turned away.

My sister did know a young man, a friend. She told him to go to the platform. He called our parents' names, and everybody cried out, "It's me, it's me!" He asked, "What are your children's names?" and there was never anybody who said "Carol and Hilda." He came back and told my sister, "Your parents are not alive." She didn't give up hope.

They even let her call to the crematorium in case they had been sent there. When you look at it in the light of day, how strange it all sounds. She thought that maybe she could have saved their lives. Our mother was forty, our father fifty, so they could work. Unfortunately, they weren't alive anymore. She had tried.

When I came I still had my little suitcase from Germany with whatever was left. You had to drop everything when you got off the transport. Everything you were carrying had to be put down fast. "Put it down! Put it down!" The old prisoners had triangles sewn on their prison clothing. Distinctive colors indicated who they were: yellow for Jews, purple for Jehovah's Witnesses who were there because they wouldn't fight in the army, red for political prisoners, pink for homosexuals, black for criminals or prostitutes. I never saw any pink.

On the platform there was a Kapo, an inmate guard, who was a Jew with a red triangle, which meant he was arrested for a political act – very unusual. He was an Austrian Jew, arrested when the Germans moved into Austria. He was arrested as a member of the socialist party rather than as a Jew. He had been in other camps and then had been transferred to Auschwitz to be a Kapo.

Since the Germans didn't want any commotion on the platform – no emotions or hysteria, everything quiet and orderly – they sent the mothers with their children to the gas chambers directly. Then there was no problem with separation. The Kapo was trying to do something to help the young women with children. He took away the children, giving them to old women so the young women could live. He thought, children will be killed anyway and the old women too. So he tried to save the young women, but they began to scream. So this didn't work out. I don't think he was killed for this, but he didn't survive. He was shot on the evacuation from Auschwitz.

We were lined up single file on the platform and they looked us over. They were in their uniforms with shiny boots and dogs, always with the dogs, but they were muzzled. They liked everything to be calm and quiet. They had riding crops and tapped their boots with them. We were made to line up, and they went down

*Rails into
Auschwitz-Birkenau*
(Picture: Sascha Feuchert)

the line signaling by hand, "This way, that way." We didn't know it, but if you went to the left, you went immediately to the gas chamber. If you went to the right, you lived, at least for the time being. I didn't appear so bad to the SS people so I was marched into the camp. It was a camp that was part of Auschwitz known as Birkenau. It was the reception area. It was August. It must have been hot, but I don't remember the temperature. The barracks were long cement structures. They were built to be horse stables.

On our way into Auschwitz, we were sent to what they called the Sauna, a processing area. It looked like a big slaughterhouse, all cement and open. They asked you to disrobe, take all your clothes off. The SS men would look you over like a bunch of cattle. They would look at our bodies and make a selection. Then came the point when they would shave your head. They lined us up. There were girls in black aprons, all Jews. As I was looking at the girls with hair clippers, I saw a girl with one arm stretched out at an odd angle. Before I could think, I called out, "Karola!," and it was my sister. We hugged and cried. We had not communicated for four years. I didn't know she was alive. She didn't know that our parents were dead. Even the SS overseer was touched.

This overseer was Irma Grese. There is a book about her entitled The Beautiful Beast. She was twenty-two when the British hanged her after the war. You can imagine how young these people were who were trained to be SS supervisors. She must have been a teenager, just about our age. She was beautiful and fearsome, quite undependable and cruel. She personally sent hundreds of thousands of people into the gas chambers.

People think that because somebody is pretty they can't be cruel, or because somebody's a woman there is an innate softness in them. They were trained not to have any tenderness in them, at least not for us. She was so beautiful and so mean that camp inmates looked at her as a vicious dog. She always had a whip with her and would hit people without reason or warning. Someone said she used to be a rider in the circus.

When I found my sister there were tears in Irma Grese's eyes. She heard us speaking German. She looked at my sister and said, "Karola." She didn't know her name, but she heard me calling "Karola." She said, "Well, you don't have to worry; your sister's going to stay with you now from now on. I will take care of your sister. She can stay with you." We were so happy we would have kissed her, the Beautiful Beast. She said she would make an exception. She said my sister wouldn't have to shave my head, just cut it short. She could pick out clothes for me. It made a big difference. All the other people were envious. My sister was even able to sneak me some bread and sugar, which I ate immediately. I was starving. Of course, we did not stay together. Grese made these promises and never kept any of them. She was emotional at that moment. She actually had tears in her eyes.

My sister directed me to a person with a black triangle, a German criminal. Even the Kapos couldn't go from barrack to barrack but would get orders signed by the SS men that they needed to get some paint or something. Sometimes the soldiers knew what was going on, but they let it happen anyway. This one particular Kapo would come with messages or food from my sister, so each of us knew the other was still alive. One day he said, "They're letting me go free." I said, "Good, congratulations." He said, "You know where they're sending me? To Stalingrad to be cannon fodder." This is what they did with the German criminals. They were sent to the front. He was a really nice guy who had killed his wife. I don't know what else he did. He was not particularly anti-Semitic. He had nothing against the Jews.

Transports came in from Hungary, thousands of people. We said they came from "Freedom" where they still had a modicum of comfort. They were well dressed. They had most of their possessions. Some of them even had fur coats. They wore fur coats to Auschwitz! It sounds ridiculous, but it's true. They had diamonds! They were thinking in terms of normal society. They thought they could trade things for necessities. They had no idea what was going to happen to them.

One of the inmate guards had been a prostitute, a very rough person. She insisted that all prisoners call her "Müttchen," little mother. The SS made her and her group examine the prisoners from Freedom. They had to examine their body cavities to see if they were hiding anything. Some of the women objected, and she said, "But I'm a woman like you."

The woman who supervised the prisoners in the barracks was called the Block Elder. All Block Elders in Birkenau were girls from Slovakia. They were the oldest prisoners. They had been there the longest. They were seventeen to twenty-two years old. The Block Elder was in charge of keeping the prisoners in the block, lining them up, making them sit down. There weren't any beds or benches. There was straw on the floor.

They would cram almost five hundred people in each block.

They lined us up in rows of five. That's how you lived, in rows of five. This is how they fit so many in. You sat down in a row and spread your legs. Then another person sat between your legs. That's how you slept. Nobody stirred or complained or yelled. If you did, they hit you with bats they carried.

The Kapo in our block made a welcome speech. She said, "This is Auschwitz. This is not a sanatorium. There is no god here; I am the god here!" I thought she was quite right. I agreed with her. There was no god there.

Food was actually better than in Lodz. The soup was thicker. We each received a tin bowl with a spoon attached. We got black coffee and bread in the morning. The Kapo gave it out, and she could help herself first so she got a bigger portion. She didn't look starved. She had a little cubby in the front with a small bed. It was much more comfortable.

We were lined up for counting. They lined us up in fives. The SS woman would give the Kapos the numbers, and they were responsible to make the numbers come out right. They would count us again and again. Then the SS woman would come and check.

It was now near the end of the war at the end of 1944. We were assigned work in Auschwitz. I was assigned to the delousing unit. When I was in the delousing commando, there was a young SS man who was my supervisor. He was about my age and from an area close to where I'm from. He talked about how Germany would win the war. He wanted to go home, but he said he was embarrassed that he hadn't been to the front. He would be embarrassed to say he spent the war with women and children. When you work, you develop a relationship, and eventually they start to see you as human. Soon you have some kind of relationship, a dangerous relationship. I said, "I hear they're burning people." You could smell the terrible smell. He said, "Who told you that?" I said, "No one told me, I just heard." "Well," he said, "no, they're burning rags."

There was one SS man who fell in love with a Jewish girl, and they ran away. They were caught, and they shot her and put him in prison. There was no rape in Auschwitz. They didn't look at us as women, but animals. It was taboo. They called it Rassenschande, race pollution.

Everything that happened, every choice you made could get someone hurt. What could you do? You could be completely passive, take no action, You couldn't do that really, so you felt responsible. But you were acting on instinct. Nobody knew, really, what would happen. Always there were selections. They were deciding who would go to a work camp.

There were two other sisters, and they wanted to stay together as my sister and I did. I was put in the group for the work camp, but my sister was at Auschwitz, and I wanted to stay. The other girl's sister was going to the work camp, so when the SS woman wasn't looking, we switched. We both wanted to switch, but who knows what happened to her?

There were so many people coming into the camps. Auschwitz had many satellite camps. My sister wanted me to stay in Auschwitz, to stay together if possible. She spoke to her friend, "Have my sister tattooed." Only Auschwitz inmates got tattooed. If you see someone with numbers tattooed, you know they were in Auschwitz. So I got tattooed.

Then they transferred me to Auschwitz One, which was the actual work camp. I don't remember what I did there. I was there two months. They did not have much work for us to do.

Berthel

There's another very moving story about my sister's friend in Auschwitz. She had known this girl from childhood. Her name was Berthel, a nickname for Bertha. Her mother came from our village, Nieder-Ohmen. I knew her. Berthel used to come and stay with us in the synagogue and play with us. She was two years older than my sister. In 1941, my sister was taken to a labor camp in Berlin. Berthel was also taken. They met there again and stayed good friends. She was equally religious, and they kept house together. They worked in different places, but at night they were together in the subways, and they talked a lot to one another. At the labor camp while she was at work, Berthel met a yeshiva bocher, a young man with a lot of Jewish learning, and she fell in love with him. She had only one wish. She was about eighteen or nineteen. She wanted to marry him. She didn't know what was going to happen, but she wanted to experience love and marriage.

The Nazis allowed her to get out of this labor camp, get a little apartment, and live there with him. She got married. She had no wedding gown, so they took the curtains off the windows, and they put them around her. She got married. Everybody gave her some pots and pans, whatever they had, and she set up house in Berlin. It was okay for half a year until they were taken to Auschwitz in 1943. My sister was taken a week before her.

A week later my sister saw Berthel on the Lagerstrasse, the camp street. Berthel was always vivacious, intelligent, and beautiful. She had always said, "We're going to make it through this. We're going to be okay. Don't worry. We listen to what they have to say. We don't make any fuss." She was always up, never down. But then one day my sister saw her sitting on the street. She was little. She was thin already. My sister said, "What's the matter?" Berthel said, "I'm pregnant, three months pregnant. I don't think I can make it. This is impossible." My sister said, "You're such a strong person. You are going to make it." She was going to give her food even though she hardly had any herself. She said, "We'll get you through." Berthel said, "It's too late already; it's too late." She said, "I have one wish. I know you're strong. You're a young girl. You're probably going to survive. Do one thing. Tell the world what they have done to us." My sister held her in her arms, and she died.

Saloniki

We called them Saloniki. They slept on the broad wooden bunks above me. All the bunks were in three tiers and meant for at least five prisoners to sleep on. If there were too many transports or an unusual number of prisoners had been left alive, we would have to make room for more or even double up.

The Salonikis were two sisters left over from one of the transports that came from their hometown by the same name. They were Sephardic Jews, the only *Sephardim* I had encountered in the world of the concentration camp. We called them Saloniki because we could not pronounce their names, or we did not want to bother with more strangeness and exotica than what we were living with all the time.

They were younger than most of us, still belonging to the forbidden age of childhood, which the Germans did not tolerate among the inmates. They were tall for their ages, though eleven or twelve, which may have been why they were kept alive for the time being. I believe I heard them tell that a *Kapo* had taken interest in them as they arrived with a transport. Most of us were in our middle or late teens, and many of us developed an almost maternal relationship to the two girls. There were incidents of shared rations, a true sacrifice indeed on a starvation diet, and cover-ups at the incessant counting and work details.

The counting sessions were particularly difficult and took place at set times throughout the days. They were to establish a continuous head count of the inmates. Since diseases, attacks of diarrhea in particular, were rampant, many found it difficult to get off their bunk and march to the counting where they were forced to stand in lines, motionless for many hours, regardless of the weather. Elaborate schemes were devised to fool either the *Kapo* or the German SS women so that those of us who were too ill to attend would not be missed.

The two Saloniki were often the beneficiaries of these deceits. In turn, they would sometimes teach snatches of Greek or Spanish, or perhaps Ladino, which sounded much like Spanish to us. They picked up Yiddish and even German very quickly and delighted some of the Polish-speakers with phrases in their language.

As Auschwitz was evacuated, I lost all contact with them. I still see their dark eyes under the shaven skulls and hear their bright voices calling down to my bunk "*Kali Mera,*" – "good morning" in Greek.

There were Sonderkommandos, special commandos. They were strong young men who were sent into the crematoria for the purpose of processing the corpses. People were told to strip naked for the showers, but in the end they were in such a hurry with the Hungarians that people went in with their clothes. The Sonderkommandos had to take the clothes off the corpses, sort them, store them, take jewelry, gold teeth. Nobody could do this for too long. After a few months, they would kill them and create new Sonderkommandos.

Then it seemed like the camp was exploding. There was a tremendous earthquake. Some girls had smuggled gunpowder in from the ammunition factory. The Sonders got ammunition from those girls and were able to blow up half the crematoria. After that they stopped the gassing. Eighteen SS men were killed. The SS men walked around with an air of total indignation. "How could they do that to our people?" Total indignation.

The girls were hanged. We had to stand all day and watch the hangings. We had watched hangings in the ghetto too.

A few girls were injured. The SS men made such a fuss. They took them to their own infirmary and bandaged them and took care of them, all because it was done by the enemy. These were "their" Jews. They could inflict damage, but they were angry if anyone else did.

Surprisingly, there were never any air attacks by the Allies on Auschwitz except once on the munitions factories outside.

By the Barbed Wire

By the barbed wire stand the soldiers
Clutching shiny rifles in their arms.
My feet are numb, but I must try to wade,
Sick and exhausted, through the muck.

Above the stretches of barbed wire
My tear-dimmed eyes
Search for the canopy of stars
That must still be above me, far above.

My frozen arms I lift,
A humble beggar, up
To the light that I have lost
As hideous horror has closed in.

By the barbed wire stands the Ancient Reaper,
Dully staring out of sunken eyes
Into the night, the cold and foggy night,
And at my silent pleading.

By the barbed wire stand the soldiers,
Watchful rifles, burning flashes –
Heavy clouds of hellish smoke
Float where still the stars must be.

My lips, turned blue and clamped in terror,
Are quivering in wild despair:
There, there, in blood-red flames
My sweet mother meets her death.

You – who high above the burning martyrs,
Above the heat of hellish flames,
Above the rifles of the soldiers
Stretch out your ever-loving arms:

Do you not hear a mother's cry of agony?
Is your ear deaf to the suffering world?
A cruel silence fills the night – and by the gate
A soldier leers a nasty grin.

My throat is raw with groaning,
My eyes are dimmed with tears,
My feet, rubbed bloody on my trek,
Are tied down in the muck.

One last time the flames leap up
In crimson fury. As they reach the clouds
They meld
Into the blazing morning light.

By the barbed wire stand the soldiers,
Watchful rifles sharp and hot.
Tightly wrapped in clouds of fog
I cower silently on the fresh ice.

Death March

They made plans to evacuate us in January 1945. It was an incredible sight as we all marched out of the gates, people streaming from all sides. Men and women were separate. Some people waved. We had to keep marching. We learned to sleep while walking. I didn't know this was possible. We would walk in threes, and people would take turns. They would prop you up in the middle and let you sleep a few minutes.

They marched us into a barn. I was afraid they would set it on fire. They did that sometimes, but they didn't this time. In the barn I found my sister again. She had a serious eye infection at that time.

For about a week we walked through the southern Polish countryside. At night we would sit in the snow. We woke up covered with snow. Anybody who fell behind or lay down got shot. The road was lined with corpses. We found out later that the death rate of the women was much lower than that of the men.

The soldiers were walking too, but eating. They brought in another group to relieve them from time to time. They were armed, and they had dogs. Eventually we were loaded on a train of coal cars. One SS man had half the car. There were seventy of us in the other half. We thought that was unfair. It really annoyed us. Girls were saying, "He has the whole half car." In the midst of all that unfairness, we resented that as much as anything. But it just shows you how the human mind works. Everything they did was unfair, but you observe the thing that you have to deal with directly. We were probably warmer all together in that half of a car.

A whole train of men had come out of Auschwitz, and there was a bit of conversation, people inquiring after certain people. We had reached a freight yard, and there was an air raid. All the SS men were diving under the platforms. It was very exciting to us. We wanted to watch some destruction, and we did.

We stopped in a camp called Ravensbrück. This had been a Nazi camp for politically active women since 1933. We stayed for four weeks while they were reorganizing, deciding what to do with us. It was a much more organized camp than Auschwitz. From there we were taken to Malchow, a small town just northeast of Berlin proper.

Remnants of survivors were coming in from the East. They took us all further into Germany. That was the astounding thing. They didn't want to leave anybody behind if they could possibly manage it. They felt it was their duty to bring all these Jews that they had been trying systematically to do away with. They wanted to hold on and do it themselves. Last-minute casualties were tremendous. In one camp, towards the very end, they loaded all of the men on a truck, put it into a barn and set it on fire. These are things they kept doing until the very end, to the last few days.

Eventually they brought us into another camp in Mecklenburg, east of Berlin. That was a labor camp. They had all these satellite camps spreading off the large camps. There were prisoner-of-war camps in the neighborhood. They had lots of English prisoners there next to us, lying around like sick dogs. They did have a little more than we did. They threw soap across the fence a few times because they got packages from the Red Cross.

At that time the German population itself was running out of food. My sister got to work in the kitchen, heating the kettles where they cooked the food. I didn't work there because I was little, but she was tall. They always wanted the big ones. The kitchen was always the best place, the source of all good stuff. It was the best place to be if you had to be in the camp. You didn't get much food, but at least you could help. She had to start a fire every morning with wet wood. It was very hard. She prayed a lot because if it didn't work they would get very angry. They would hit you and beat you.

Food was practically nonexistent. They cooked potato peels and oatmeal, a little oatmeal, but no salt because we had no salt. Whatever salt they had went to the soldiers. Whatever little we had, there was no salt on it. We got thinner and thinner and weaker and weaker. People were already weakened by the time they got there. There was no crematorium in the last camp, but we died. People just died. My sister managed to get a little bit of soup out of the kitchen for me.

Martha got some sugar. That was another friend of my sister's who had been in Auschwitz. She also came from Germany. My sister has two friends that were her camp sisters. I don't have any of those people because I was always alone. The people that I came in with, they were all gone.

Martha worked in some kind of supply house where they gave her rubber boots because she was standing in water most of the time. She came into the bunk where we were sleeping. She whispered to us, "I brought sugar. I brought sugar!" The rubber boots were filled with sugar. Naked feet in there with the sugar, but it didn't bother us. We were happy she brought sugar. We had not seen sugar in years. She sat on her bed, and she said, "Pull my boots off." All the other people heard. They said, "What does she have there? Martha, what do you have?" She said, "I brought a little salt. I have terrible arthritis, and they gave me a little salt. Here, you want to lick it?" Because she figured salt they didn't want, but sugar, everybody there would have licked her feet. It was sugar, and she gave us the sugar, and we ate whatever we could. She wanted to share with everybody. She was such a good-natured person. There was just enough for the few of us. We took the sugar and ate it. It was stuck to her feet, her wet feet. We really didn't care. We licked her feet. It was like a holiday for us. We were so happy! We were so hungry, and all we talked about was food. Just like in Lodz.

We went through Berlin where we saw to our great pleasure how they had bombed Berlin. All concentration camps were emptied out so survivors and the disintegrating German army poured out onto the same roads. There were a tremendous number of SS who had lost their jobs and who finally had to admit to themselves they were losing the war. Until the very last moment the Nazis did not want to believe they were losing. They made counterattacks on the western front. It was obvious they were beaten, but they did not want to admit it. The Russians were coming. There were as many SS men as there were of us, thousands of SS men.

All they did the last few weeks was drink to numb themselves. They had a good time, but they kept themselves unconscious and they shot a lot. They had weapons, and they became dangerous in a different sort of way. They were shooting across the whole campgrounds. The last days, they just sat on their bunks, drinking and firing their guns. We just hid under the bunks.

Then some of them got civilian clothes and tried to blend into the population. They just went away. Some of them were probably caught.

We were liberated in the woods. Suddenly, the Nazis disappeared, and we were left in the woods.

Free At Last

As soon as we were liberated, it was one big Kaddish. *We said the prayer that is said for mourning when someone dies. One big* Kaddish *went up to heaven. Everybody said* Kaddish *all over the place. We said* Kaddish *for ourselves really. It was like we had been in a deep and dark hole. There was no sun coming through. There was no life, and we had gotten out suddenly, at least some of us did, to a place that was entirely different. We talked about others coming from "civilization." We talked as if they were coming from a different country. We didn't even talk about which country geographically. We talked about "civilization," a country where people lived normally, as civilians. We didn't see ourselves as civilians, just as inmates.*

Our final guards were not SS anymore. They were reserve soldiers akin to the National Guard. They wore military uniforms but without SS insignia.

In the last day or two the International Red Cross appeared. We had never seen them before. They came in big trucks accompanied by Red Cross ambulances. In Lodz I had seen ambulances with Red Cross markings before, but those served a different purpose. The Germans took people to the gas chambers in those ambulances. I was scared of the ambulances. This time they turned out to be genuine Red Cross ambulances, and they had food and soap. Soap was a big issue – and chocolate. Why did they think we needed chocolate so badly?

A few days before they had brought in rations. The soldiers had taken them for themselves. Later they threw these rations at us. People would grab whatever they could. That was the only outside help we ever had. We were later asked many times: "Didn't the Red Cross ever come in?" No, they didn't. They probably were not allowed in. Prisoners of war did receive rations. They had that advantage. The Germans took everything from us because they were hungry themselves.

We were liberated in the woods. The time was early May 1945. A tank pulled up with three Americans in it. We were sitting there as the tank rolled in. It was high, and the Americans threw down chocolates and such. Survivors streamed in from all sides. There were so many survivors that we didn't get any chocolates. Then, as we were walking down the street out of the woods, we saw a jeep. One of our group asked the Americans which way to go. They said, "Follow us. Hitler is dead. Follow us. You're free!"

We were caught between two armies, the Russians approaching from the east and the Americans from the west. We were in the middle, in no man's land. There were a lot of white flags that had been hoisted by the Germans.

The Nazis had told the population to evacuate. People had no place to go. One could see many people, some in open horse-drawn hay wagons. These were the farmers. They loaded up all their household goods on these wagons, and they were trying to go someplace. They had left their homes, and now they were on the road. They were together with us and with the remnants of the army. The army was marching, trying to get to the American side to avoid being taken prisoner by the Russians. The Russians had a fearful reputation.

There were also SS on the road, but we didn't know who they were. They blended in. I remember some concentration camp survivors, men who had taken the uniform off dead SS soldiers. Several of those got themselves killed that way.

We had come out of the long tunnel of night and stood bewildered and blinking in the new light. We had come off an alien landscape inhabited by monsters. There was no easy re-entry. The post-war terrain in Europe was only vaguely familiar. Most of the old markings had been lost. Our family was gone. We had no home, no country. We were "Displaced Persons." That was the terminology used at that time to identify people like us.

I kept saying to my sister, "We're free, we're free." She said "Yeah, we are free, but we have no place to go." We were kids. There was no home anymore. There were no parents, no relatives. We were stateless and homeless. There was no food, no clothing, nothing. We were just two kids.

We ended up in a potato field and started to roast some potatoes. As we were sitting in the field, a guy came by on a bicycle. He stopped, looked at us, and said, "Where are you girls going?" We said, "We don't know. We're not worried anymore. We're free now." He said, "You don't recognize me?" We said, "No." He said, "I'm the commandant of Malchow." Without the boots and the uniform, he looked like any other guy on a bicycle. As the commandant he appeared to be eight feet tall. Now he was five-foot-eight. He said, "You know you were with us during the war, and the Russians won't like that. You better go to the Americans."

We thought, "What is he talking about? Did we cooperate with the Germans?" That was the implication. I said nothing. Others said, "We're not afraid of the Russians." Maybe we should have been, but we were ready to welcome them with open arms.

We found ourselves in a barn exhausted with excitement and fatigue. We went up in a hayloft, and I talked to two English soldiers the whole night. They had slaughtered pigs and roasted their flesh in huge bonfires, using straw and firewood found in an abandoned farm. Whatever they stuffed in my mouth, I swallowed, absolutely everything, and everything came up again. I became violently ill and threw up the whole half-digested mess. This was the first time in four years that I had enough in my stomach to throw up. We slept. We were sick. We slept and ate the whole night.

The next morning we looked out of our hayloft, and there were the Russians. Russians were all around us. They were our liberators. They ignored us at first. The next night we went into a farmhouse, which the owners had evacuated. We slept in feather beds – clean, white beds.

Some of our girls stole bicycles for us. We also had a covered wagon. There was a Pole who was supposed to protect us. He sold us to the Russians for a bottle of whiskey. The wagon had two horses. The Russians kept exchanging the horses. They would bring us new horses and take ours. We were finally left with one lame horse to travel through a good part of Germany.

The Russians had the worst-equipped army. While Germany had a modern army, half of the Russian solders had their feet wrapped in rags. They seemed largely illiterate and ill-fed. To be sure they had motorized equipment, but we saw mostly horses and wagons. It's amazing to imagine that they won the war. They lost millions of people and have to be given credit for withstanding Hitler.

The Russians were not easy to live with. They were angry at the Germans, and they did rape and pillage. We had a lot of trouble with the Russians, who didn't know who we were. They had a hard time making a distinction between us and all the others on the road, their enemies. What did they know about survivors?

The Russian army was given permission to rape any woman. There were times when we slept on top of roofs because we were afraid, but we escaped. We met a Jewish army officer, an American. He advised, if ever a Russian soldier would approach us, we should start coughing and tell him that we had tuberculosis.

Americans were not a problem. They would try, but we'd say, "No way!" All we had to say was, "I'm not feeling well," and they would leave us alone. They didn't want to rape, just have a good time. Russian soldiers were different. They acted like animals.

There was one situation involving a Slovak girl who got friendly with a Russian major. He was Jewish. She ran away with him.

The Russians insisted that we drink with them because if one did not drink with them, they felt rejected. We practiced all kinds of tricks to pour the drinks out.

One time an officer got drunk and went to sleep. A Slovak girl took his gun to make sure that he didn't make trouble while drunk. He came back the next morning looking for his gun and for that girl. He could not find his gun and was fit to be tied. To lose one's weapon was a major infraction of military conduct, punishable by death. There would be no court-martial. He would be shot. Punishment would be administered on the spot.

We met another Jewish soldier who spoke Yiddish. Among his comrades he didn't want it known that he was a Jew. Then he cried. Russians appeared to be very volatile. They would dance and sing and get extremely tearful. They would drink some more, get wild, and break into song.

So this is a Jew who spoke Yiddish, and he realized we were Jews. He called us Shvesterle (sisters), kissed us all, and said he had lost all his family. He also told us that he could not protect us from the others because he was a Jew and that they were very suspicious of him. For the first time I got a sense that Russian Jews weren't so well off in Russia, that they had to hide being Jews, that it was not a comfortable life for them, and that they had to be on guard. Among the other Russian soldiers their position was precarious.

People immediately seemed to separate by nationality. People kept asking, "Where do you want to go? Where are you going?" Most didn't know where they wanted to go. They formed national cliques. We didn't have any clique to go with. We didn't want to stay in Germany. We happened to be in Germany, but we had no intention of going back to our home. We were the only German Jews. We ended up with the Slovak girls. There were twelve or thirteen of those girls.

The Russians gathered together different nationalities to repatriate to different countries. There was this one girl from Dobšina, in Slovakia, whose name was Stern just like ours. She had lost her two sisters and wanted to take us to her parents, though she didn't know if they were still alive. She wanted to take us home as her substitute sisters. We told the Russians we had Slovak citizenship, and they didn't care. They put us on a train going south.

It was a cattle train, old cattle wagons, which they kept open. They didn't shut them on us. It was fun. We went all over. It was different because the atmosphere had totally changed, but also because we were away from the Russians. A lot of prisoners of war piled into those cars.

That's how we got to know the Serbian partisans, partisani. Our political point of view was formed on that trip. The Serbs were really friendly, and they told us in whatever language we could understand how much they hated the Germans, how they had fought them during the whole war. They also told us that the Croats were pro-Hitler. Understandably, sympathies for a long time have been with the Serbs. They had caused a lot of atrocities too, but they were good fighters. They fought the Germans as much as anyone. Many of them were killed, and many of them were taken prisoners of war. They were the lucky ones that were prisoners of war and didn't end up in concentration camps.

At some railroad stations they fixed up a shower for us where they normally washed down the cars. There was a tremendous gush of water that came down. People rigged up a stove right in the train. We got bread from the Russians, heavy black bread.

We finally got farther south to Slovakia. Our special Slovak friend had gotten a message that her parents were alive. Her father came to get us. Some older Jews were still alive in Dobšina. The Nazis had taken all the younger people, but her brother was still there. We went up into the mountains, the Carpathian Mountains. The countryside was beautiful. It gave us such an elevating, wonderful feeling. We didn't know anything about our future, if we had a future, or what we were going to do. All we knew was that we were free. We didn't want to worry.

The Jews in Dobšina took us in and gave us food and clothing. The mayor declared us honorary citizens. My sister still has that certificate. She had been with the Slovaks in Auschwitz for so many years that she spoke the language. I just went along with her. She told the mayor that she was born in Frankfurt, that her father came from Czechoslovakia. That's why she spoke so well. We wanted to survive so we made up a story. If we had told the truth, we wouldn't have gotten anywhere.

We stayed about three weeks until we realized that there was no life for us in Dobšina. A couple of guys were going to Bratislava, the capital city of Slovakia. We went with them. All the bridges had been blown up by the Germans. We walked and went by wagon again. Sometimes people gave us rides, and after some time we got to our destination. That's where we encountered the Russians again.

At one point, we were in a room with a lot of elderly women and men. We were in what had been a Jewish community center in Bratislava. Russian soldiers came in, and these older women said, "Why do you bother us? Why don't you take the younger girls? You have the young girls." They were pointing them to us, and we started to cough. We put up a storm, and they left us alone. Nobody touched us because of the coughing.

We went across the border. The border was a railroad track between Slovakia and Austria. We wanted to go to Austria, so we stood on the Slovakian border. That was the Russian zone of Austria, and the Russians kept shooting at us. We said to the Russian soldiers that we were from Austria and had a father in Austria and that we wanted to see him. He asked us who we were. Now we looked like Gypsies so Carol said "Zigeuner," which meant Gypsy. She looked very much like a Gypsy. Her hair had grown long and was black and dirty. She said, "That's my little sister, and we're Gypsies, and we want to go to Austria. Don't shoot, don't shoot."

He said, "Well I'm not going to shoot. I'll let you go." There was a demarcation line in Austria. He said, "I'll let you go, but when you cross the border you still have the Americans to cope with." It was early in the morning, five o'clock. The Americans were fast asleep. We didn't see any Americans. We didn't see anything.

We stopped at the train station and saw some other survivors there. We recognized each other by the way we looked, saying "chaverim," comrades. They told us they would take us along to a displaced-persons camp, a DP Camp. On the way, many times, we slept on the ground in railroad stations. We were truly homeless people. We didn't mind. We didn't care because we were free.

When we were in Vienna we went to a public bath. It was like a palace, all marble inside. They had two deep baths that one steps down into, like a mikveh, a Jewish ritual bath. They brought us towels. There was an attendant in there, and they treated us like royalty. We had gotten some Kronen, Czechoslovakian money, from a Jewish organization called the JOINT, the Joint Distribution Committee. That was the first money we had, so we paid for the bath. We felt so luxurious. My sister was sitting in one bathtub and I in the other. We waved at each other. It felt so good. It was heaven on earth. That was our sightseeing trip. We didn't go to any of the castles or anything. We just wanted to be in that bath. It was so nice.

We had tried several times to cross the demarcation line to get to the DP camp. They wouldn't let us across. A whole bunch of people wanted to cross. We tried several times to cross, and the Russians caught us every time. There was a train going across the line that was full of Austrians. People even hung on the outside. We approached the Russian soldiers and asked whether we could go on the train. We showed the numbers tattooed on our arms. One soldier took us, and he chased out all the Austrians. But then we realized that maybe he thought we owed him something after that. He sat across from us for a while, but then he did get off. We were very relieved.

We met more and more survivors. They were the ones who told us where to go, what we should do, and we listened to them. It was sort of a network. We could immediately get established. Eventually, we got through that second, very difficult border, and once we were in the American zone everything went well. That's when American soldiers approached us. We told them the story with the little English we spoke. We tried to tell them that we were survivors. They were very good to us. That's how we got into the DP Camp. We were liberated on May 3rd, just a few days before Armistice, and we must have gotten into Austria, to Kammer-Schörfling, about September. The whole summer we struggled, getting from one place to another.

We had nothing to carry with us, just whatever we had on our backs. Somebody gave us a royal blue slip, one slip between the two of us, a full-length slip. We finally got in a DP Camp, which had been a Jewish home that had been taken over. It was beautifully located on a lake and even had a boathouse, a gorgeous place. The DP's invaded it completely and made it their own. I don't know if the owners ever got it back. Downstairs was a Czech man with two children who occupied most of the house. We had a room upstairs. He was a very nice man. His wife had *been killed. A maid was with him, an Austrian. The maid was so good to his children. We ended up in the maid's quarters. It was a tiny place with two beds right next to each other. My sister took all our possessions and rolled them up in the royal blue slip and put it there. Wasn't that a beautiful pillow? We always made everything look nice.*

It Matters Who I Am

Oh no, what matters now is not that I can speak,
It matters who I am.
No words, only the quest for answers
Can give a meaning to my being and my state.

She who bore me, thrusting me into a world of woe,
Bequeathed to me with her last gaze
Her torment. All my questions now
Have one by one been wrapped into her memory.

As clouds disperse in novel patterns,
So do I write myself into the sky
Instead of all the words that burn within me
And that I cannot understand.

A Letter to Aunt Erna, mother's sister in New York (Fall 1945)

Today I hope to be clear-minded enough to give you a detailed report of my life and experiences till I finally reached Kammer-Schörfling in Austria, where we are now. All those atrocities are so fresh in my mind that it is hard to put them on paper in a clear and cold report.

Let me start from the beginning.

When other children used to play to lose themselves in the nonsense and happiness of childhood, we had to hide and evade the growing and officially created hostility of other children and grown-ups. We never knew what it meant to live our lives free. Then came the terrible time when we had to leave everything.

In February 1941, Karola, my sister, was sent to Berlin and was forced to work in a Siemens-Schuckert ammunition plant. She was not yet 16. My parents and I were "evacuated" in October 1941 to the Ghetto of Litzmannstadt (Lodz).

It is impossible to write of the agonies both during the transport and after arrival where we endured temperatures far below zero in dirty vermin- and typhoid-infested, dilapidated shacks. But above all there was the terrible hunger. The memories of these living corpses will never be erased from the minds of the survivors.

Over a million Jews from Germany, Poland, and Czechoslovakia were killed in the gas chambers of Lublin and the terror camps of Auschwitz. There were four gas chambers and crematoria in Auschwitz to burn the more-or-less dead. In the end they burned the children alive because of lack of gas.

Karola was sent to Auschwitz in 1943 in a transport of two thousand men, women, and children. Of the two thousand, only four, including Karola, survived. From the transport in which my parents and I were sent to Poland I am, to the best of my knowledge, the only woman among only three survivors. The fact that both of us are alive is one of the most miraculous and unimaginable occurrences.

When I was sent to Auschwitz in the middle of 1944, I met Karola, who was forced to be a "hairdresser" in the large undressing hall where all were shorn. We had to dispose of our clothing entirely. We got dirty rags and walked barefoot in wooden shoes. Our life consisted of endless roll calls in the mud and in the cold under continuous barbaric treatment and beatings.

Finally, in January 1945, before the Russians took Auschwitz, the Nazis brought us under terrible hardship to Malchow on the Baltic Sea. We were liberated there in May 1945.

Karola and I hiked and rode through the almost impassable Russian Zone for two months until we reached the American Zone. Now we have been in Kammer-Schörfling, near Salzburg, for two months.

You can imagine that it seemed to be heaven after all the sufferings and hardships, finally to have found a roof and a place, and above all human beings with a human heart. We don't know how long it will last and are still poorly equipped and without sufficient shoes and clothing.

Our most urgent need are shoes (size 7-7 1/2), underwear, stockings, dresses, and coats. In short, everything. We are now wearing uniforms fitted for us. You can imagine that we would like to look like presentable human beings again, so that we can get away a little from the past, although we can never forget it.

Bits of Sweetness

The bits of sweetness that give zest to life
Turn to gall in my mouth,
For I still cling to
The heavy walls of Yesterday
And listen to the muffled echo of the drops of time.

Today is just a groan
Cowering at my feet,
But lo and behold!
I think I will last until tomorrow.

The Day Is Blind

The day is blind and dreams descend
Into the deeper waking that is not yet sleep.
Old trees are smiling at me from afar,
They know that I am older still than they.

Rain clatters on their turgid leaves
Still shiny from the early morning's sun.
Raindrops jump jauntily in all the gutters –
And I am young, young as the rain.

They Tell Me

They tell me that the world's a round contraption,
a little pin set on a stretch of bowling lane.
They tell me that I am a brightly colored Nothing,
a will o' the wisp that gives no light.

And so I must believe that death is the deep source,
the darkest part of Being that gives food to Life;
for if the deep did not provide for life above,
the brightly colored Nothing that gives proof of Being
would not be.

I Open Wide My Arms

I open wide my arms toward the vast
Quiet sky that sheds its warmth on me.
The unborn joy in my poor heart
Purrs like a kitten when it licks its fur.

My hunger-hardened limbs rest heavily,
Uneasily among the tiny flowers,
When bits of songs creep to me from the bushes
Their drab old dresses stained with blossom-blood.

Covered with yellow dust, their hair pulled out,
They pant as they squat down around me:
How will I now make songs from little scraps
When I don't know what they are all about?

Displaced Persons, a story

To the left of the entrance to the Displaced Persons' Camp was the Director's office. Out of a sudden feeling of distress, I went in. The room was small and narrow, and a folding cot almost filled it completely. Young fellows and girls were standing and sitting around in the self-absorbed immobility that is always ready to jump up and run, a state that sometimes appears in the immediate aftermath of severe suffering.

These people were feared and hated throughout the region, for many of them went in for stealing and robbing. They were filled with a fierce need to acquire, to amass, to collect, to cheat, and to take revenge, endless revenge for the violation of their youth, for the shame visited on their bodies and their souls. Yet much of their time was spent in a state of mindless torpor.

The director was a blond boy with nice blue eyes in a coarsely cut face. His mistress sat next to him, a nineteen-year-old girl, brown-skinned with a pretty, expressionless face and a body filled with broad expanses of flesh. He called her "Kitty-cat," and indeed she was always snuggled up to him, purring like a fat little cat.

Many were talking, although the words did not come close to any meaning. Perhaps the sensation of speaking was pleasing to some of them, but what was being said was little more than a kind of idiomatic hodgepodge.

Eventually, someone started belting out a Russian song in rough tones and others joined in, their voices abruptly starting up only to break off in boredom before long. Darkness descends, and no one's eyes here shelter dreams, only the jolts of repressed pain that we jealously withhold from others – from those on the outside.

Here we feel community, and some of us begin to breathe heavily. We are loud in our secrets, but we do not hate ourselves for the noise of our silent desires. Hate is located on a higher plane, and it only meets itself when resignation has been dissolved.

One fellow goes outside, and he cannot prevent me from following him. It is not often that the cry of the owl is heard in September nights; perhaps it announces vengeance to the lamplight that aggressively protrudes here and there.

The fellow outside squints at the moon, which, in its yellow mistrust, barely emerges from the clouds. The young man's skinny limbs rattle as he turns his body right and left, waiting, with his eyes and the corners of his mouth pulled up in puzzlement. Within him stirs greedy desire, the wizened changeling that hunger has left behind in him.

One senses that the fields are near. They probably bear stubble from which no grain was ever cut or grass that has withered before it was mown. Darkness has added shadows to the trees. Midway on the hillside the air becomes moister, but further down it presses heavily and forebodingly, mysteriously filled with smoky and sweetish smells.

And then we pick up the hostile and unfamiliar scent of a house. An open window next to the ground gapes like a wound that time has forgotten to close. Behind it in an invisible corner, a wooden bed awakens, disturbed by the tossing of a sweltering body.

Across the bare floor come steps, dragging, irritated, sleepy at first, then expectantly picking up, and finally stopping in disappointment. Two faces meet in the window frame – that of the girl white and bloated with faded-looking eyes; that of the fellow dark and strangely furrowed, greed showing white between thin lips and madness laughing in feverish eyes.

Pity and contempt are in her voice when she asks, "Are you looking for something?"

She pronounces the words in the heavy, overly distinct manner in which one speaks to children and foreigners. She wears a large, shiny watch on her wrist and tries to hide the panic that suddenly seizes her. Was it the greed that jumped out of his eyes like a yellow cat? Was it the contemptuous, rag-clad hatred that roamed the nights trying to appease its hunger for warmth and shininess that overwhelmed her within a second?

Enough! Either way, it was too late. Grabbing her shoulders with his arms, he vaults into her room with one nimble jump. It is upon him again, that accursed, insane vision: Big, white, blond women with heavy breasts well molded in gray uniforms … playfully caressing shiny boots with shiny whips … their wide pockets filled with jingling gold … strong and proud as they strut between long unending rows of men, and women too, whose very essence they have sucked from their limbs.

I do not know what happened, but I saw the shiny watch for a long time, saw it in the light of the moon, which now stood big and liberated in the sky, awakened perhaps by shame. The young fellow dropped out of the window paler than ever, but his lips were a brighter red from the rare feeling of vengeance enjoyed.

Later, he may have noticed me among the trees, but only in the camp did he come close enough to laugh and try to take me by the arm in embarrassed haste. As I inquisitively looked into his eyes, he quickly let go of me and sullenly grumbled, "Oh I see, you are one of ours. You all might show a little more gratitude for the revenge we take; in part it's for you!"

I did not answer and instead hurried off to my shack.

What We Have Lost

Before us, with an easy smile, was
The world, wearing the bright garment of our youth.
We never thought to probe with furrowed brow
What life might have – or not – in store for us.

Around us were our walls and homes and fields,
Our earth of rich black loam,
And high above the verdant green of forests
Appeared the rays of our brilliant sun.

But now that the walls have fallen in
And forests, uprooted, stare into the void,
Now that the world has sunk into blood and darkness,
We who remain are undone.

What we have lost is life,
What we have lost is death –
All that remains is emptiness.

Letter to the International Red Cross

Attn: Miss Balk
Linz
HQ Military Government

Since our liberation from the concentration camps six months have passed. Six months we have waited and heard the most varied promises. Several times already we attempted to make our most elementary needs heard, but without success.

Now we have decided to present our situation in writing. In Chiemsee Camp III, set up for displaced persons in general, there are currently captives, some four-hundred-fifty persons strong.

Much has been written about us and is still being written; much more was promised to us. With the exception of the one-time receipt of food packages, we have unfortunately received nothing. Our situation is, in light of the oncoming winter, a very critical one, and it remains to be feared that the small remainder who succeeded in escaping the murderous hands of Hitler must succumb to the newer conditions.

We are completely without provisions and suffer a lack of even the most rudimentary clothing. Our women own no undergarments, not to mention any warmer clothing for winter. Were the morning and evening counts not missing, the forced labor and the mass graves, one could assume that nothing had changed.

I believe that we need not repeat that that which has occurred to us has no match in the annals of history, that we were robbed of all our possessions, that we were treated in a manner never before seen – that any description would be too banal.

We beg not to be categorized under the soulless and stereotypical term "DP," displaced persons. Rather that we, who have suffered terribly for five years, who possess no home any longer, or at least may not return to one, be treated accordingly.

In particular, if the letter from President Truman is to have shown any current value at all, we ask for additional clothing and food since our health, after many years of concentration-camp stays, requires particular attention.

Should you not believe our statements, we request you to convince yourself of the state of affairs through a personal inspection. In light of the fact that a delay of our concern would mean extensive damage to the health of those in question, we request an urgent addressing of the same.

My Truth

At first I held my tongue, a silent beggar,
But now I'll have my say, demand the truth.
The shilly-shallying of all the others
Makes me so desperate to be heard.

When I was knocking at a thousand doors,
A hundred opened just a crack;
But wide enough to let me enter
None of them, none was opened up.

Here and there I gathered bits and pieces
And stored them in my hiding place.
They make a cunning little nest
For little eggs my song has laid.

At first I held my tongue, a silent beggar –
But listen here, I'll hatch these eggs,
And from the nest of lying bits and pieces
I'll push the naked truth when it has hatched.

Then let it find food on your doorsteps,
Pick little crumbs until it fledges out.
Meanwhile I will lie low where I have hidden
Until you murder it, the fledgling truth.

Gmunden, March 3, 1946

My Dear Ones,

Just the other day we received a package with yarn, curlers, floor polish, and food. With the same mail delivery, we received a very nice package from Julius Salz and sometime before that a little package from Diablo, California from Flora Flensberg, née Andern and a letter from the Halberstams.

From Diablo we got, oddly enough, only soap. Apparently they think it is a good object to sell here.

At any rate, we are always glad to hear from our relatives and acquaintances and are always happy to feel the many instances of well-intended and empathetic assistance around us.

In and of itself the term "home" and all the German "humbug" and all that goes with it, which has been applied to us, has become quite foreign – and yet the heart's warmth of those beyond the Atlantic has flowed over to us and conveyed in a friendly fashion the forgotten and yet so often painfully missed feeling of being "at home." For that we are better; a just Destiny will thank you all for eternity.

Our beloved and never-forgotten dead, who like so few were actually buried in the soil of Poland before my very eyes, are already with you in spirit as they are with us. They are for us, beneath their abandoned graves in the cold earth of Poland, the great call of warning to that which is true in life, to the human, the really human heart.

There is much talk of the Jewish heart. There may be something true to it. It would be better if one came gradually to the realization that each human is made up of the same substance. Here's to war being eradicated from the world and that unnecessary tears would finally cease to flow.

I am rather melancholy today because at this time two years ago we lost our Mama.

We no longer live in one household with the Pretzbergers. We cook for ourselves, that is, Karola cooks. We have many poor acquaintances, also former inmates, whom we sometimes invite because the comradeship remained after that intense time of need. The Pretzbergers don't understand that and will never understand that. They are typical cold-hearted people who have suffered too little. I know that you all understand us better. They should not think they are getting short shrift because of us.

Kisses to you from

Your Hilda

Hilda on the Traunsee, the lake in Gmunden in Upper Austria, in 1946.

Time Has Slipped Away

My head is pounding with the stifling heat,
The sultriness has put my will to sleep.
Leaves do not move, tree trunks are sweating,
And from the clouds the sun takes aim.

Such days are hard to bear with equanimity,
They press upon me like a sweet and sticky vice;
I do not want to meet their challenges
And take to my cool bed of worrydom.

And so I worry: time has simply slipped away,
And still is slipping fast and faster.
No one has started anything – I'm no exception –
And yet we all have reached the end.

It was very hard for us to trust anybody – very difficult. After the war a lot of people in Austria came to us with all kinds of sad stories. They wanted to legitimize themselves, claiming even that they were Jews, in some cases telling us stories that they were really on our side and not on the other side. They wanted to get legitimacy with the occupation forces, the Americans. We had some key words that we would ask them. If they didn't know them, we knew it was a sham. In many cases it was. It's amazing what people will tell you when they think it will work to their advantage. Some of those people may have been trying to gain an advantage, or they may have actually been guilty of something or other.

Right after the war when we had been liberated, and Germany was under American occupation, we wanted to emigrate to the United States. The American consul demanded that we get our birth certificates. I didn't know how to accomplish that. There were some friends, Jewish friends, in the American army, who were also of German-Jewish parentage. They had come to the U.S. right before the war. They told us that they could connect us with the local civilian telephone lines. At that time almost all local utility services were still struggling under the effects of the war.

I called up my village. I got through, and I said to whoever answered me on the other phone, "This is Hilde Stern and Karola Stern. Remember me?" And there was dead silence on the other end. They called somebody else, somebody who had become mayor since then. He said, "Karola and Hilde! Where are you? What happened to you?" I got very angry. I said, "You ought to know what happened to us." I wasn't very nice at that time. He said, "What happened to your parents?" I said, "They're dead. You killed them all!" They were very, very unhappy with my talking to them like that. I said, "I want nothing from you. All I want from you is my birth certificate. Send it here." And they did.

Liberty boats transported troops back to the United States. On the same boats they also transported back Germans who had American citizenship but had elected, just before the war, sometime in the 1930's, to go back to Germany because they were friends of Hitler. They were Nazis, a lot of them, and they went over, and now after the war they could claim their American citizenship and come back. They came back with us. We were together on those boats. I remember standing in line with them for food. They turned to us and talked to us. They told us that they were sorry to see us there and they were sorry that we were alive. I remember that very clearly. We actually complained to American officers about that, and they said, "Well, you know, don't make a big fuss about it." They had no feelings for this. They didn't really understand. They knew we had been in some oppressed situation. That was pretty clear. But they didn't understand. Except for the ones, possibly, who actually liberated the camps. Their lives had been changed forever.

Soldiers stationed in Germany had a good time with the German girls. They were trading cigarettes and chocolate for sexual favors. They didn't have to rape the girls. They came voluntarily. The soldiers had a wonderful time. Many of them didn't want to leave Germany. It is a very seductive country, also unfortunately for Jews. Very few German Jews went back to live there. Now there are Russian Jews there, many with children who were born in Germany and who speak flawless German. There are quite a few Israelis who went to Germany to live there. Who would want to go back there?

Hope

My hope is for tomorrow,
Easy days,
For sleep and for the fleecy cloud
That gently carries me to dreams devoid of fright.

I suffered hunger,
Lived upon my flesh,
Friends found me by the wayside,
And friends make me forget my yesterdays.

I eat my fill,
I walk in ease,
I like myself and I like others too –
And yet I wait for better days.

My hope is for tomorrow,
Soundless nights.
My deepest hope is for a God
To walk with me and show me how to travel
The hopeless path.

Hoffnung

Ich hoff' auf morgen,
hoff' auf leichte Tage,
hoff' auf den Schlaf und auf die Lämmerwolke,
die mich durch Träume schrecklos, sanfte trage.

Gehungert hab' ich,
selbst mich aufgefressen,
und Freunde haben mich am Weg gefunden
und Freunde lassen gestern mich vergessen.

Ich eß' mich satt,
ich schreite ohne Plage
und seh' mich selbst und andre mir gefallen
und dennoch warte ich auf beßre Tage.

Ich hoff' auf morgen,
hoff' auf Nacht und Schweigen
und hoff' auf einen Gott, der mit mir wandert,
um mir den hoffnungslosen Weg zu zeigen.

In America

When I first came out of the concentration camp, I kept saying that we're all human, and I was all-forgiving. After that I looked at some of my own poems. I was really horrified at some of them because they were so depressing, so terribly depressing. After I read the poems, I was really down. I really felt terribly low. My eyes were focused on human depravity, all human depravity. Today I have some considerable distance from it, but it's still really raw. I despised humanity. I felt like I was submerged in mud. It was this kind of feeling, like it was some gush of mud and dirt that just covered the world. Of course, it was the only world I saw, and we were together there with all the murderers. We were together with them down there in the mud. It's dehumanizing. I felt that for a couple of years afterwards.

Then I wrote another poem. That was a year after I got married in 1948.

Spring Time

When thin dust borne on blue wind
Hovers outside the window I have shunned too long
New stalks and pussy willows tell me
That I have sat too long in wintry houses.

Let me go out: then will the dust disperse,
Then will the wind air out the rooms,
Then will a shallow life find depth again
And new abundance fill the space of emptiness.

Frühling

Ein dünner Staub, von blauem Wind getragen,
hängt vor dem Fenster, das ich lang vergaß,
die Stengel und die Weidenkätzchen sagen,
daß ich zu lang in Winterhäusern saß.

Laß' mich hinaus, damit der Staub verschwindet,
damit der Wind die Stuben lüften kann,
damit das Seichte neue Tiefen findet
und neue Fülle, was so leer begann.

You can see distinct hope in that one, sort of a reawakening. But I kept a distance. Nevertheless, I felt somehow implicated in the mud. We were all there, both soldiers and the prisoners, except for the people who were dead. Everybody who survived – and this is so common among survivors I would say it's universal – we all have that awful feeling of guilt – guilt simply because one survived. I always feel guilty about everything. It's very easy to make me feel guilty. People take advantage of that, of course. It's very easy to make me feel guilty. I think that's true of all survivors. They have a feeling of guilt about everything. In their families, whatever goes wrong, they think it's their fault somehow.

I came to Baltimore because we had family here, cousins of my father who were born in this country. They were willing to take one of us, either my sister or me. I wanted to see what was out there, and I came to Baltimore to live with total strangers. I was very lucky. Very shortly afterwards, I met my husband.

My husband was a graduate student. At that time in the post-war period, most of the students were going to school on the GI Bill of Rights. Many of them were married. So here I was exposed to a lot of non-Jews from various parts of the United States. I had absolutely nothing in common with them, except for one woman who came from Armenia. Her parents had been in the forced march imposed by the Turks, and she empathized. She had a feeling for me. When she told about her parents' experience, I felt quite close to her. She was the only person who I could have anything in common with. It never even occurred to me to tell the others. They wouldn't have known what I was talking about.

I was out there in the world from the very beginning after the war, and I made an adjustment. I immigrated into this country. I became part of both the non-Jewish and the Jewish parts of it.

There are very few German-Jewish survivors. Mostly, when you think of a survivor, you think of Hungarians, Poles or other Eastern-European Jews. There are very few German-Jewish survivors.

When my husband met me he didn't believe I was from Germany because both my sister and I had adopted sort of a Slovak Esperanto. We picked up an accent from our non-German-Jewish friends. They spoke German, but they spoke it with a very distinct Eastern or Austro-Hungarian-Empire flavor. The pure German accent, I thought, was associated with the Nazi enemy.

And so we sounded like Slovakian girls. For many years, that's how we spoke. It sounded very different from somebody who was a native German speaker. It took me a while to get back to my native accent.

My husband had been in England for several years. I had made a decision that I wasn't going to marry a real survivor, because

I realized that I would never be able to get my head above water. I felt such a separation from the rest of society and wanted somebody who knew what it was all about, who understood at least; but I did not want somebody who actually went through the same thing.

My husband fit the bill. He had lost his parents and knew what had happened. He needed a home as much as I did. I had a need to live a bourgeois life. Kids are usually rebellious and want something different from all the rules and regulations of the stultifying lives their parents lived. That was the case with the kids in the 60's and the 70's. I would have been that way myself if I had had a normal life. So I looked at the settled life of the bourgeoisie, and I liked it. I wanted it for myself.

,

Joachim, a story

They met on a soggy November night. America loomed large. Blood and tearing anguish were behind them and the sum of European disillusionment heavy in their souls.

They were soon tramping the streets together to walk off American Saturday nights, the greed of manufacture, the emptiness of gasoline stations, and the pain of shoulder slaps. They had come across a gaping abyss fearlessly and felt defeated by safety.

His eyes were blue with a golden ring circling the pupil. The long eyelashes gave a childish and tender shade. Farther down, the chin was straight and edgy. She knew that she had been looking for him, that his image had emerged with his reality out of layers upon layers of instinct and belief.

She lived with a maiden aunt, an old woman, by some standards well preserved and vivacious, but in a magazine sort of way. She was highly suspicious of Else's outlandish absentmindedness, which was not as without purpose as it seemed. The things the girl uttered were ridiculously honest and shocking, in an un-American way. The worst of all was that she seemed without gratitude and accepted "the things you did for her" in a callous, unresponsive manner, "as if she expected it."

Else was thinking of God. She was a childish girl really, not a woman at all. She was thinking that He had led her out of *Mizraim*, out of Egypt, into the land of her fathers. She tried to understand, stubbornly. There was a clue to it all. Sometimes, many times before, she had perceived the red thread that had crept through her life marking the steppingstones across disaster, leaving dead and dying on the way.

Her aunt was a good woman. She was an American. She was nice. She did not want her, but there she was.

"A way to make a living" was Else's first American revelation. Once the understanding had taken hold of her, there was no resentment. She prayed and opened her eyes. America was a great shiny mirror, a powerful, superficial reflection, and she was to study her image as pictured therein.

Joachim went to seek his woman. His handsome, soldierly face was closed and stony. He hated the new country. He hated the past countries. He hated the dead and the living. He hated the dust of books and the stench of laboratories. He was young and relentless and menacing. He was trying to grow older. So Joachim went out to seek the woman. She was thin of limb, feline and subservient. She was great and noble and distant. She was virtue and vice. She was the ghost of beautiful centuries past. She was between him and "the land of our fathers."

Else and Joachim became friends. He pitied her unhappy, unlovely little figure, the hand-me-down rags she wore so unbecomingly, and he winced at her dreams, which showed in her eyes unabashedly. Civilization was not a puzzle to him, and he tried to cushion the painful little stabs that she had to expect sooner or later. The struggle was long and fierce.

Sun and sand, water and a mass of naked people covered this part of the continent. The mirror stood higher and shinier. They saw that some merriment was real, and there was less hypocrisy among naked bodies. There was the giggle of young girls and slender boys parading their clean physiques.

She prayed. She had to defeat "The Woman."

Joachim took her to a dance. He was surprisingly graceful and suave. Else was clumsy and had never set foot on a dance floor. She had hoped that he might kiss her, overwhelmed, if not by her, by the heat of the house, their closeness and possibly by sympathy. He kept aloof and entirely to himself. The laboratory was calling him back with the challenge of a lonely fight, uphill and full of hurdles.

The mirror told her about clothes, about grace, about superficial polish, and it became relevant to her, a task that had to be accomplished at once and with flourish. She had a long way to go.

After their marriage Joachim's eyes grew bluer and the circles around his pupils more golden. The pain was going out of his dreams, and some grass was growing near America's empty gas stations.

September 5, 1948 – Wedding Party with Uncles, Aunts and Cousins.
Hilda is standing in the center with Carol directly behind her.

First Wedding Anniversary

We've now been wed
for one whole year
And you, it seems to me,
Have put up with me quite well.

On the contrary, and on second thought,
If I am a Xantippe
Then You are sweet Socrates,
Who was fated from this bitter cup to sip.

Many women far and wide
May have taken it remiss
That dear God has chosen you
For this particular Miss.

You were pulled, you sank,
Such was your destiny,
And oh how wonderful it was
To be wed under that canopy.

The world is bright; sunshine everywhere
The soul can recover
With love and concern
You have made the whole world so warm
I thank God that He has found you for me.

Nun haben wir den Ehestand ein
ganzes Jahr getragen
und Du hast mich, so scheint es mir,
nicht allzu schlecht vertragen.

Im Gegenteil, und im Betracht
für eine der Xanthippen,
bist du der liebe Sokrates,
den bitteren Kelch zu nippen.

Ob auch die Frauen, fern und nah,
es übel aufgenommen,
Du bist direkt vom lieben Gott
mir in den Weg gekommen.

Halb zieht man ihn, halb sinkt er hin –
so ist es denn geschehen,
und ach, es war so zauberhaft.
zum Standesamt zu gehen.

Die Welt ist hell, die Sonne lacht,
die Seele kann gesunden –
Du hast mit Liebe und Bedacht
die ganze Welt so warm gemacht
ich danke Gott, dass Er Dich mir gefunden.

Translation: Werner V. Cohen

When we were married and lived in a basement, I thought I had reached the epitome of anything that could be achieved in life. I was very happy with my basement apartment. Every next step seemed such a powerful improvement over where I had been before. My husband could never understand my total lack of ambition. I had no ambition whatsoever.

When our kids were born, my husband wanted to go camping and do exciting things. I said, "I did it. I had it. I don't want it. I don't want to sleep on any floor, any ground." I did not want to rough it at all. I just don't want it. I know what it feels like. I wanted to have a real boring life, no excitement.

Now I Want Children

*A*t first, I didn't want children because I was so scared of kids. I only thought of death in connection with children. It took me several years till I could work up to the point when I said, "I want children." I remember saying that: "Now I want children." I wanted a family. I wanted children.

It was after my oldest daughter was brought to me in the hospital and I looked at her that I said, "Here is a Jewish child. She will never know her grandparents, any one of them. How do I treat a Jewish child after all that? How do I treat her?" I blessed her in just the same way our parents had blessed us. There is a blessing you say over your girl children, usually on Friday night. "May God make you like Sarah, Rebecca, Rachel, and Leah. May God bless you and keep you. May God enlighten his face and be gracious unto you. May God lift up his face towards you and give you peace." That was my first real connection back, back to home. Then I remembered all the Hebrew blessings, and it came right back to me.

Memories of what I had learned in Frankfurt and Würzburg came flooding back. I strengthened myself and my family. My daughter was to grow up as a Jew, to be a link in a strong and holy chain. Hitler was not to be given a posthumous victory.

Hilda with Eldest Daughter – 1953

It was about five or six years after my children were born that I regained any interest in organized religion. I never really lost my faith, my belief in God, but I felt betrayed and had problems for a long time in that respect. I wanted to go back to tradition as far as possible. That's one part, the one aspect of our married lives where I had unrelenting leadership. My goal became clear. I searched for a Jewish connection wherever I was. I've been the fanatic in the family all along and properly so. My kids took that next and final step. They are all very observant.

My faith had been shaken. Although there always seemed to have remained a strong core, my relationship to Torah and mitzvahs (the commandments) having been severed through the exigencies of the recent past, was difficult to re-establish. The continuity was gone and so was the community that had provided it.

At that time in the 1950's I looked at the society around me, and I realized I could not nourish, I could not sustain a Jewish family as I wanted it. I felt that was my task: To have Jewish children. It would have to be up to me to complete the link or at least to add another one. Fortunately, with God's help, I have been very successful in the most unlikely places. As the children grew up we never lived in any place with much of a Jewish presence.

It was difficult. While there were Jewish communities, they were not of the kind that encouraged observance. Intermarriage was common. I encouraged my three daughters to participate in whatever Jewish activities there were. They were really active, fortunately. I had very little rebellion from them. They were not allowed to date non-Jewish boys. They never did. So they had a strictly Jewish social life. Maybe that is true of more Holocaust survivors' children. They very often have a loyalty to their parents. They had nothing to rebel against. It was the sixties and seventies, but whom are they rebelling against? They knew we had been so much worse off than they could ever imagine. They knew they were lucky that they had what they had. I'm sure it's not easy to grow up as the child of a survivor.

I had my three daughters in four years. The youngest became the most assertively Jewish. It started when she went to Chattanooga High School. Chattanooga is in the South, in the Bible Belt. For non-Jews it is like a yeshiva town, for they have Baptist colleges there. One can hardly have somebody, a workman, come into your house to paint your wall or do something else who isn't going to try to convert you. It's a constant thing. Our youngest, like all my children, went to public school. There was a girl in our carpool who always traveled with her Bible turned to the New Testament in the back seat. My daughter started to take the Chumash, the Hebrew Bible, and it became the "War of the Bibles."

Fortunately, I have a very good relationship with my daughters. They see me as their mother. I mean, we're not pals. They are respectful, but we feel very close to each other. They talk easily with me.

They tell me about complaints they have now about when they were young and all the things I did wrong. And I just refer them to their own children to make sure they don't do any of those things. Don't make my mistakes. You have to find your own. Most Holocaust survivors are not observant, although there is a large group that is.

I've noticed that the children of the survivors don't try to interject themselves between their parents and the rest of the society. I've read how in earlier days of immigration the children became like substitute parents. They felt they were called upon to help acclimatize their parents into this new world. Many survivors' children felt: "My parents went through so much more. I shouldn't interfere. They probably know as much as I do, and somehow they'll work it out." The survivors were immigrants who had to struggle with the same problems as earlier immigrants, with language, work, and making a living.

A New Life

We had a party yesterday. The women were all so puffed up, so polished, but their age could not be hidden. All these old comrades of mine, wearing their Auschwitz tattoos confidently, why are they so eagerly competing in the "schmatte," clothing, department? What embarrassing decay are they trying to cover? I want them to be unvarnished, take off their gold chains and red nail polish, their new hairdos and overly fashionable clothes and be themselves, or at least, what I think is them. They are the same under all the gook. What is it; what has become of us?

Oh, Give Me Just One Hour

Oh, give me just one hour
When I can laugh
And savor happily that we are free,
For what these fools make of their freedom
Brings me despair
And pulls me back behind the bars.

Some survivors tended to project themselves heavily onto their children. It's an everyday thing. You sit down for dinner, and the child doesn't want to eat. You hear yourself say, "I wish I had had that." Something always comes up. I went through a period where I stood in front of the kitchen sink and tears would run down my face. For a long time I had flashbacks. At that time I didn't know about flashbacks. After the Vietnam War I got a whole new vocabulary. I stood there, and my mind would be entirely somewhere else. I'd visualize things, very real, in front of me, and I'd start to cry. My kids knew that. They saw that and didn't say a word. One of them still tells me today, "I couldn't even talk to you. You never heard me. Mom, you never heard me."

I remember we were at a neighbor's swimming pool. Mine were the only kids that always called out, "Mom! Mom!" The other kids did their thing, not paying attention to their mother or whoever was watching them. My children would call to me every few minutes. I think they had to summon me from someplace. They had to reassure themselves I was really there. Survivors tended to be overly protective of their children. That was not always good.

Flashbacks

A survivor was asked where she lives. She said, "I don't live here. I live in Theresienstadt." To some extent that is true. It's not totally true, thank God. I have a rich and satisfying present, but it's also very true that part of the time, I don't live here. It's a constant experience. It's always there. It has become better over the years. It's not like it used to be when I was younger, when I used to stand in front of my sink, when my kids were little, and tears used to run down my face. "Flashbacks," they call it, but I didn't know that word then. Flashbacks.

It's like a big burden. You talk about it, and you share it, but you don't take it off. It's still there. You want to share it, but somehow it comes back even more heavily sometimes. And so for me it's never a finished story. Never. I know that's hard to comprehend. It's not like a trauma that you can alleviate.

When I *daven* – when I pray – I pray in Hebrew and know most of the prayers by heart. There is then something like a film that runs in the background. I see pictures while I am praying. They catapult into each other like a film or a kaleidoscope. I don't know why that should just happen during praying, but it's there.

In the following story, juxtaposed realities involve flashbacks (shown in italics) and present-day scenes of a dying woman in a hospital:

Her eyes and the skin of her face were golden yellow, and there were maps of blue and purple on the fleshy exposure of her upper arms and thighs.

They were standing in the dark doorways, shoulders hunched down, heads hanging, arms hanging, bellies pregnant with hunger. Their teeth came forward, as if their lips had shrunk away.

She asked me how I was. She told me that she hated to receive cards with hard-to-read signatures. It made it difficult to answer them. Her son, the difficult seventeen-year-old, had bought an old car for four hundred dollars. It would be good experience for him to learn about the economics of driving, the responsibility of maintaining a vehicle, and caring for something, if not someone, so close to his heart.

They were always carrying spoons; they shuffled with feet in untied shoes. Their clothes were much too large, and they wore all they possessed on their shrunken frames. They did not talk, and they did not answer when spoken to.

Flowers brought by the visitors were placed into make-shift vases, empty honey jars, cans without their top lids and with content advertising printed all over them. The aide placed them on the large windowsill. There was one bunch of pink carnations and baby's breath which had faded to a dingy yellow-gray, and the stems looked dry. "How lovely," she said but didn't smile.

This one tall, fair-haired lady had come with us from Frankfurt on a "German Transport" to the ghetto of Lodz, Poland. She and her dead husband had been quartered in the living room which our kitchen had been meant to serve. The earlier Lodz occupants, a man and his now-dead wife, had not been asked whether they wanted to share their habitation. They could stay or leave as they liked but chose to stay.

The tall German lady had started to swell around her eyes. Her cheeks took on a hangdog look. "I think I am starting to get diarrhea, and I will use the bucket on the veranda," she said and smiled apologetically.

"I will not be here for the weekend," said the aide, "so I better take your menu order now," as she handed her the yellow sheet with the menu choices printed on it. "I am getting personal cafeteria food, now," E. said with a smile.
"Lobster gratin sounds good, and I'd love some fresh peaches."
"They inserted a Hickman catheter, and it caused a lot of bleeding, but it will be easier now to give me platelets, as I need them, without having to probe around for nonexistent veins. I just have to learn how to irrigate the catheter."

The tall, fair-haired German lady lay on the floor, and it was wet all around her. "Stay here," she softly told me, "I like you to stay with me." She didn't talk anymore. Her legs were swollen from the ankles to the knees. She turned her head to the balcony and just lay there. The man on the bed, the original occupant, said, "She's dying, but what's the difference, we are all going to die."

The local Reform rabbi conducted the Evening Service in the house of the mourners. The Reform movement uses its own updated version of the traditional liturgy. It follows the order of the service but is much shorter and made "relevant" to modern worshippers. It does not praise the Lord for receiving the dead, but rather for reviving them. I believe the mourners would rather pray for receiving the dead.

The fair-haired lady was dying slowly and calmly. Her request to remain near her gave me some disquiet, but I wanted to give the impression of valor to the native in the bed and stayed. She became very quiet, motionless, but her eyes were open, fixed on the ragged balcony with the bucket.

Since I was sitting in an uncomfortable crouch near her on the floor, I shifted position and almost fell on top of her. She did not move. "She is dead," I thought, "and I will have to close her eyes." The lids felt smooth and still quite warm and were not difficult to move. "She is dead," I told the man in bed. "We'll have to report it to the Ordnungsdienst officials." "Wait a few days," he said. "We can collect rations on her identity card." "She will start swelling," said my mother, sadly. "It's cold enough," said the man, "she will last a few days."

Her son is seventeen years old, and he is wearing a sleeveless jacket and an earring in one ear. His hair is cut short but standing up straight and spiky on top of his head. He is crying, as is her seventy-year-old father. The father is sobbing loudly and various people are hugging them, alternately. The father has taken off his shoes and is walking around in stocking feet. He remembers this is a traditional custom of mourning. Someone has covered the mirror.

She had many friends. She collected people at work, at the hospital, at the schools, which had, reluctantly, offered their facilities for her son's erratic education. Her nature was invincibly upbeat, positive, and relentlessly optimistic. She needed the medical insurance which was tied into her wage packet. She worked right up until her last illness.

The grave diggers did come the next day. I don't remember who called them. The tall, fair-haired lady was buried in Marysin with all the others.

There was no religious ceremony.

Meeting again with 82-year-old Conrad Carle (and, on the left, his daughter-in-law) in 1986, some 58 years after the former neighbor's wedding, which Hilda attended in 1928 (see photograph, page 21)

Revisiting the Past

*T*he only time that I went to Germany, I went back to the village where I was born. My class, the same age group that I went to school with until I was eleven, have up until this day a very close relationship among themselves. Some of the men had been killed during the war, and some died of natural causes. So I came. They arranged to have their usual monthly session, and they had me as a guest of honor. They asked me what would I eat, and I told them I would only eat cottage cheese and potatoes, cooked in the skin. Some of them had memories of Jews following their dietary laws. They were very happy to accommodate me.

We were sitting at a long, rectangular table, and most of them I didn't remember at all. I did remember a couple of them who were childhood friends of ours. They came to me, and they told me about all the people who were still Nazis. When I left on this trip to Germany, my sister said, "Ask for Emma." Emma was a very good friend of my sister, one she was close with as a little girl. I asked the people there, "What happened to Emma?" "You don't want to talk to her. You want nothing to do with her," they said. Her father was a Nazi, one of the early ones, and they said I shouldn't even bring her a greeting.

Everybody in that village knows each other and knows their history. There is no way to hide. They know exactly how much of a Nazi everyone was. Were you just a little bit? How committed were you to the party? They know about each other, and there's a great deal of suspicion to this very day.

That's why it was uncomfortable for me to be there again. The past is really in front of your eyes. You know the changes that happened, how open they were to the propaganda in spite of knowing better. There were a lot of people who knew better.

As I was sitting at the table, right alongside me were a man and a woman, husband and wife. The man suddenly moved very close to me, and he said, "Hilde, I want to tell you something." He started to sort of whisper. Very hesitatingly, it came out that he needed to tell me something. He said, "During the war I was in Auschwitz. I wasn't in the SS. I was a soldier in the army." I knew that there were no soldiers in Auschwitz. Any German in Auschwitz was in the SS. But I won't give you my interpretation, I'll just tell you what he said: "There was barbed wire around the men's camp. One of my army comrades came to me and said, 'Where are you from?' I told him from a village called Nieder-Ohmen. 'Ah-hah,' he said, 'There's somebody here from Nieder-Ohmen, a Jude, a Jew. Come here, come, you can see him.' And so this man comes up to me, and he's just a skeleton. I looked at him, and I said to him, 'Siegbert, is that you?' And this Siegbert, he says to me, 'Yeah, I am. That's me and I just hope that the day will come that you will be here and I will be out there.'" That's what he said.

I just sat there and kept looking right down at the table. I wished I could have sunk under the floor. He knew that my reaction was not good. His wife grabbed him by the arm and dragged him out of the room, and they all looked at me. The man who he mentioned was somebody who had come to Lodz. I didn't even know he had ended up in Auschwitz. Obvi-ously, he didn't survive. The one who told me this story was somebody who very likely had been an SS man. He had something on his conscience, and he had to tell me that after all these years. If he had kept his mouth shut, it would have been just as good for me. I think he wanted me to give him absolution, to say that I understood or something like that.

I also saw Otto, the one who I had played with. I was the queen, and he was my king. He was quite a nice-looking man. He came all dressed up, and I said, "Where is your wife?" Somebody said, "He didn't bring his wife. He wanted to see you." I didn't know whether to be embarrassed. He hugged me and kissed me. He remembered our games together. He probably was in the German army. I don't know what his standing was.

All these things were just hovering there, like ghosts. We were all very civil and nice to each other, but the room was full of these ghosts. A few people were very sincere. With one of the women, I had been very friendly. She told me of all the people who still were Nazis.

1986: Hilda returns to visit Nieder-Ohmen

About Faith

The night right after we were liberated, I got to a house where I had the opportunity to tell two soldiers about everything that had happened – really tell it all night long. I think that was a smart thing. It was some instinct I had, and that seems to have given me a head start other people might not have had.

That's the sort of thing that happens. You can't predict or plan for it. I didn't know anything about Freud. I had never heard the name before. It had nothing to do with modern psychology. It was something that just happened. I felt the need and the anger, the need to tell about what had been done to us.

It was already the end of the war, and so I felt free, not threatened. I took a chance. They were perfect strangers. The initial unburdening that I did at that time has stood me in good stead ever since. I can't really explain it, but I seem to be pretty healthy psychologically.

I've always been happy. It's my basic faith that I do believe, still believe, in humanity. I feel that there is a great deal of good in many people, maybe in most people. They have asked me, "How did your faith in God survive?" I don't think I ever lost it. I was very angry. I permitted myself to be angry at God, and I never felt that was wrong. I had no fear of being angry. I said, "How can You do that to us?" And because there was no answer, I finally came to the realization that God was really in the camps with us, that for every person who died and suffered, God was also dying and suffering with us.

I had this distinct feeling that God was with us, and everybody else represented the other side, the devil. It felt like the Nazis were non-human. There was something in them that was demonic. We were the human, the good side that was being persecuted. We stood for all the good in the world. That's my perception of it. It had very little to do with rituals. And I felt I did not owe any rituals anymore.

The Germans now seem to have an obsession for the Jews that were there once, not with Jews that are. The Germans always had their archaeologists digging up the past. They've long been documenting things from the ancient East and different parts of the world, but now they're digging us up, and we're still alive. I'm not even sure if I should be offended by it or flattered. It's a puzzle. I would say, "So why don't you concern yourselves with the Jews who are there now? Do they have an opportunity to live a full Jewish life? Do you promote them in living a Jewish life? Is that of interest to you, or are you only interested in what happened in times gone by when you buried us all?"

In Judaism there is a teaching that every deed, the good or the bad, has its own reward and somehow gets reflected back. This sounds very reality-based, people hurt and people destroyed. God knows I can't place blame. Don't tell me that it's our fault. If somebody says that, I will get angry because it's ridiculous. Very wonderful people were killed. There is a Hasidic mystical notion which is very compatible with what I believe. It's called Tsim Tsum, the withdrawal of God. Somehow we caused God to withdraw from us; not you or I, but mankind. God sometimes withdraws, because mankind becomes corrupt.

Even so, man is a creature, he or she. They were created by the word of God. The creatures have their choice. Choice is always given. Sometimes the choice goes too far in the wrong direction. That's when Tsim Tsum occurs. In other words, it's given to man to bring God closer or chase Him away. So in a way, we drive God out of the world, and we also bring Him back. It is given to us to choose, and there is reward and punishment in that sense.

Jews have a mission. The whole notion of Tsim Tsum is focused on us. We have a role to play. The hope is that we go forward in the right way so that we can bring salvation to the world. This is really our mission. That's why we suffer so much, more than anybody else. It's painful. A statement, like saying "I'm Jewish" ten times or a hundred times, means nothing. You may say you are very proudly Jewish and would never hide it, which some people do. It's only a statement without substance. One has got to live it! By living as a Jew you know you make it real in your life. It takes every last bit you have to live as a Jew. It's not an easy matter.

Well, it's very easy actually, once you're in it. I know that it is very difficult to start from the outside. It takes a real commitment. It takes a total commitment.

I think we should be held to a high standard. Whenever a Jew does something wrong, other people will take note. Other Jews will feel embarrassed too. They take responsibility, and that's not a bad thing, although it has not helped us very much. There is an expression – al kiddush HaShem, sanctifying the Name of God. Al kiddush HaShem is a standard by which you can live. I think the real meaning of al kiddush HaShem is that Jews are, in fact, held to a higher standard, and most of them resent being held to that standard. It's very understandable.

Everyone who died in the Holocaust died in a state of al kiddush HaShem. Many people were quite removed from actual observance, but they died as Jews, for no other reason. Because of that they did die al kiddush HaShem. When people ask me why did it happen, I don't have any answer for that. There are some things that cannot be answered.

Judaism teaches about forgiveness. If you sin against God, that's between you and God. If on the other hand, you know you sinned or did something wrong to another person, God will not have to forgive you for that. It is for you to make up to the injured person. You have to ask for forgiveness from the person you harmed.

There has been no revenge, and there's never going to be any revenge, but I don't have the right to forgive the murder of our parents. It's for my parents to do that. My parents are gone, so they can't forgive. I cannot forgive the murderers. I'm not asking for revenge. Maybe they're gone. Maybe they're dead. I don't even know who they are. There were too many of them. We don't believe in turning the other cheek. We don't expect to love our neighbor more than ourselves. We can't even manage to love them as much as ourselves.

When I first came to Baltimore, a poetry-reading session was featured on a radio station at 11:30 at night for fifteen minutes. I met someone who had a connection to that radio station. This man looked at my poems. He liked them, and he translated some of them and had them read on the program. I didn't enjoy it. I didn't want anything to do with it. The people I was staying with, cousins of my father, seemed pleased, but I didn't feel I wanted to share. I felt it was very private, and it really wasn't anybody's business. I didn't do it to become famous. I felt very private at that time.

Right after the Holocaust, people didn't want to hear anything about it. That's how it was until the late 1970's. People weren't interested in me or anybody else telling them about it. My elderly American cousins, the ones I was staying with, said, "Oh, what a shame." That was the end of the conversation. I didn't know much English, and these people did not know any German. I lived with them for nine months. It was not easy for me. I met other ladies who were full of self-congratulations every time they shipped some used clothing to people like me in the DP camps. I was not deeply impressed with their rabbi. He stood so far removed from what I knew to be the truth. It just wasn't Judaism, as I knew it. It was a weak imitation of Protestantism. It had all started in Germany in the early 1800's and was called Reform Judaism. It was claimed that there was poor decorum in the Orthodox synagogues. Reformers wanted to have an organ and all the trimmings of the Protestant church.

There had been other movements that had spun off from traditional Judaism, but until the nineteenth century everybody was Orthodox. Reform Judaism is basically a German, then American phenomenon. Traditional Judaism is so varied and so rich with so many different shapes and forms. I think any Jew can find a home there.

Musings

I have returned from an orgy of nurture, submerged in the flesh of the young grandchildren, my heart warmed by their eyes, sparkling and eager.

My children came home to me, women now, vigorous and capable and prepared to carry on. I did the cooking and much of the laundry, unending. Days flowing one into another, picking up the little ones, reading stories, fondling, caressing and playing, keeping them from harm, hour after hour, their mothers grateful for relief, much as I might have been when they were little.

The grandchildren are all at different stages – infants, toddlers and pre-schoolers just starting out into that never-ending pursuit of book learning.

The early development of personhood has been the subject of innumerable and ever growing studies and treatises. Learned lifetimes have been devoted to mine the subterrain of childhood.

But there is nothing to compare with the miracle of holding and nurturing a young child. All of the wonders of the world are contained in a gurgle or satisfied burp. When one's arms are full with the warmth of a baby, there is no emptiness in the heart.

Out there in Auschwitz they had large heaps of children's shoes, children's clothes. They threw the children into Red Cross trucks in Lodz to be sent to easier camps, they said.

All the children left in Lodz were shrunk into their rags. They may have never fitted into them before, but now they were even larger. The children always were little beggars, carrying their spoons and little pots and hanging around street corners asking for food. Everyone was hungry. Who had food for them?

My grandchildren are well nourished, thank the Lord. They are well cared for. It took me years to get ready for motherhood. It seemed such a precarious state. They might take the little ones away, or how could I make up to them all the deprivation suffered in Lodz and in Auschwitz? I wanted them to be normal and not have to stare down into an abyss.

Today I went grocery shopping through the canyons of packaged and canned food and past the small partitioned fields of vegetables. A sentence from the prophets flits through my mind. "*Yeshurun* waxed fat and kicked."

Hunger is abstract in America. I heard in the news that a Congressman disguised himself as a "Street Person" and mingled with those who are unfortunate for real to find out what their life is like. He did not enjoy it, but will use the experience gained in the legislature to seek improvements in the lot of the "Bums."

Thoughts Toss Me Back and Forth

Thoughts toss me back and forth; I cannot sleep,
Although I long for deep forgetfulness.
Yet high above me still they stand, the kind old,
Always kind and watchful stars.

I have the information, know they might hold worlds,
I also know that each of them reduces me to naught.
"The heavens proclaim the glory of God," 'tis said,
But I hold on to my earth, hold tight.

Wandering above me too are clouds, bluish chimeras
With long wings such as gods of legends sport;
Yet I do know that they yield only water,
More rain to fall into the quiet pond.

So many images, and so horribly disjointed
That hand can never hold, nor finger follow them.
Restlessness here below and silence high above –
A cloud bursts into tears, and I weep with it.

The car broke down. It wouldn't start. It happened in the parking lot of the supermarket. It's humiliating to have to cope with two recalcitrant tons of steel, and I don't feel less human or female to despise the contraptions of our age, while nevertheless having come to depend on them.

Thinking about age gaps gives a sense of futility. Is there such a thing as an "age ghetto?" In the 1960's, the term "Generation Gap" had come into vogue, and while the hullabaloo associated with gender liberation and "Panthers" of various hue has softened to a murmur and only an occasional shriek, the age segregation has not vanished.

The young also have been fenced together in corrals of educational institutions, the young adults into downtown office buildings and restored gentrification to generate taxes and upward mobility, the middle-aged into suburban strongholds of conservatism and family stability, and the elderly into a vast arid field of leisure pursuits and poverty.

Years ago, my mind would catch sparks like fireflies and hurl itself into a poem, an exultation. The need for the sparks still exists, but the exultation is too fleeting. It may take a different force to gather the creative energy needed for producing the work. Slowly gathering my resources may in the end help me to move towards my goal, which has escaped me all my life. The discipline needed will require surrender of freedom, surrender of ego, surrender of the flittering outside of me. Page by page, I will have to chain myself to hand and pen and block out all the incoherent shadow thoughts, the long mashed-down anxieties and nightmares, the disgusts and demons. They all need to be spewed forth – to clear out the garbage.

HaShem, the Almighty, will support me in this perilous trek and not let me fall off the path. Whatever nonsense may escape from my imagination, which is just painfully beginning to let down its guards, may it be for the good.

Hilda in 1985

Last Photo of Hilda – with Husband, Daughters,
one Son-in-Law, and Grandchildren –
June 1997

I want people to know more than the facts of what happened. People get served up a lot of facts. I want people to understand the human beings involved, to see how it impacts in our everyday life. How if we feel quite honestly, ruthlessly honest about this, we have to realize the potential of the average human being. We don't look at it clear-eyed enough. We're not humble enough. You can say, "This can never happen." Well it can happen. There is a potential. You can walk to the abyss, which is within yourself, and look into it and say, "Oh my God, I can't believe it; this is not me." But I have that in me too. This humanity that we all share is for each and every one of us to deal with, to look at, then to transform, to make into something that's noble. That's each and every human being's mission. Many people don't achieve that.

Look at what happened. Some people were willing to put their lives on the line. That's what some of those people did in the Holocaust. In some cases people sacrificed their own lives helping somebody else; and for the people who couldn't do that, there is an understanding of their humanity.

People say education will transform you. It does not necessarily transform you. When people talk about growth, they usually talk about it in terms of intellectual achievement. You have to grow, but there are many aspects, spiritual and moral. There is a moral potential. That's the one we should explore and try to grow.

One cannot teach Judaism based on the Shoah, *the* Holocaust, *and Israel. It's much more than that. People are desperately looking for other content, when it's all available. They just have to look. It's all there. It's not difficult; yet still I'm worried.*

Survival of the Jewish people is very meaningful. It's the most meaningful thing to me. When I look at my family I feel there's a sense of survival and satisfaction. I don't know if they're all going to carry it on. I hope they will. I believe they will. It's a triumph over all that evil that was done to us. That's why I have struggled to teach Hebrew school. I think even if you only save one soul, you feel like you have done something.

We won. Hitler is dead. We are still here. We have three Jewish children and twelve Jewish grandchildren, and Hitler is dead.

We won.

A Daughter's Loving Portrait

by Deborah Cohen Katz

Some have "met" my mother, Hilda Stern Cohen, in the frame of her Holocaust experience. The Holocaust ended when she was 21 years old. During the fifty-one years that followed until her death in 1997, she lived a full life in America. She was aware and grateful for the daily gift of life itself.

Mom started life in the small farm village of Nieder-Ohmen. Others have described the details of her idyllic childhood. But what stands out as a lifelong theme that started in childhood was her independent spirit. From an early age, young Hilda took criticism from well-intentioned relatives who worried she wouldn't succeed in life. Yet she did not cease to bury herself in her beloved books. Early on, Mom had remarkable clarity about who she was and demonstrated the courage to provide for herself emotionally and spiritually.

Mom found a way to set an emotional balance point that served her well throughout her life. A kind of emotional duality emerged. She was part of her village community, yet not exactly of it. She was self-disciplined, but very flexible. She needed privacy, yet she was happy to be with people. She observed life unsentimentally, but she was neither humorless nor uncompassionate. She took herself seriously, yet she laughed easily at her own limitations and foibles. This ability to embrace opposite character traits within her personality without judging them gave her immense emotional and spiritual resilience and integrity.

Hitler rose to power in Germany in 1933 when young Hilda was 9 years old. Within a few years Jewish children had been evicted from the public schools. In 1937 Mom obtained a space at the Würzburg Teachers Seminary. The decision had been made by the school to admit younger students in order to permit them to continue their education. Mom blossomed intellectually, emotionally, and spiritually. She developed a formidable understanding of the philosophical and theological foundations of Judaism through textual study of the Torah giants, in the original Hebrew. Yet the most astounding achievement of this thirteen-year-old girl is that, in a mere year and a half, Mom had developed a mature concept of God, one that protected her through the dark years that were soon to follow and one that profoundly shaped the rest of her life and the lives of her children and grandchildren.

During the war years that followed, 1939-1945, my mother lived through the nightmare now referred to as the Holocaust. Despite the many traumatic events of those years, Mom did not give in to the emotional and physical agonies that consumed virtually everyone around her. Her father had taught her that though the Germans could kill her, they could not control her mind. She chose to observe with objectivity and great compassion the reactions of other Jews around her. She was in the Holocaust, but somehow never of it. In those years her understanding of basic human nature reached maturity.

My mother met my father, Werner Cohen, in 1946, shortly after they each had arrived in Baltimore as new immigrants. My father was my mother's ideal choice for a husband because he understood the trauma of the persecutions she had suffered but had not himself been in the camps. They both yearned for a home and a sense of normalcy. They married in 1948. Three daughters were born to them in quick succession: Hedy, Debbie, and Michele. Over the next twenty-five years they raised their daughters in middle-class America, determined to give them a healthy childhood. Most important to them was a commitment to look to the future, avoiding much reference to the trauma of their past. They decided not to speak German in their household. Hilda, the poet, consciously chose to disinherit the language of her art.

America was a strange place. In the wake of Mom's Holocaust experience, American life seemed vacuous to her. She had no time for Madison Avenue. She did not buy into upward mobility. She did not share the pervasive sense of entitlement. The joys of material gain were, at best, insubstantial.

By 1960 Mom had decided to begin to create a religiously observant Jewish home for her family. She constructed a religious family environment without the advantage of an established Jewish community infrastructure. In the various small towns in which we lived, the family observed the Jewish Sabbath alone. Remarkably, all of the daughters became strongly identified with the Jewish faith and the Jewish people and grew up to raise ritually observant families of their own.

Mom became a religious-school teacher in every city in which her family lived. Her commitment to Jewish continuity extended to all Jews, especially children. She had an answer for Hitler: The Jewish People will not die. She resolved that she would try to rekindle as many Jewish souls as possible, teaching them about the Jewish God. These rekindled Jewish souls, she hoped, would be a living memorial for all the others who had died, *al kiddush HaShem*, as Jewish martyrs. Mom was an intensely private person, yet she clearly saw her mission. She committed herself to cultivating and renewing Jewish vigor in America through Jewish education.

Mom seemed to know God very well. She talked of a loving, caring, and, above all, a forgiving God. She never saw God as responsible for man-made suffering. *Tsim Tsum* is the concept that, by limiting His Presence in the world, God created man's free will. Because God "stands back," He lets man decide whether to choose good or to choose evil. This choice is a trial every person must confront many times in life. Mom understood that God did not create the Nazi crematoria. That was *b'chirah*, human choice. In the middle of Lodz, even in Auschwitz, my mother felt God's presence. He was with her, crying, right there with her and her people.

Mom had a deep understanding of what it meant to be human: our nearly divine capacity for goodness and likewise our propensity, without much resistance, to participate in evil if

it is properly packaged. She understood clearly the nature of self deception – how we learn to hide the motivations for actions even from ourselves – and how we allow ourselves to do things we had once believed we could never do. Mom also understood the importance of forgiveness in a practical way. She intuited that by being consumed by anger and hatred for the Nazis, she would hand them a posthumous victory. So she chose to detach herself from the anger and go on with her life.

In some respects, my parents' marital relationship was a coming together of opposites. Yet their relationship was an outstanding example of *shalom bayis*, family harmony. Both of them were unequivocally committed to marriage and family and believed in doing the hard work it took to keep a family strong. They didn't expect marriage to be easy. They didn't expect life to be easy. And, as a couple, they were able to ground their relationship in a bond of trust and mutual respect.

In the late 1980's, my parents returned to Baltimore in retirement. There they enjoyed a decade of life together in a large, well-established Jewish community. Mom took great satisfaction in watching her children and grandchildren grow, knowing she had accomplished something important with her life. She absorbed herself in Judaic studies and Hebrew-language study and spoke to groups, whenever asked, about her Holocaust experience.

In the communities in which they lived, Mom came to be respected by many for her formidable grasp of a wide variety of subjects, her intellectual honesty, her well-considered opinions, and, above all, her deep, uncomplicated humanity. Her greatness was in her humility, her keen discernment of human nature, and her unswerving commitment to God, the Jewish people and her family. Rabbi Leonard Gewirtz of Wilmington, Delaware wrote: "She lived through the Holocaust and her own lamentations. Through all that, she sought and found in the strength of her soul the ways to overcome the Job-ian questions and to come forth as a woman of faith and courage. She inspired all who were touched by her, and she brought the learning of her youth to her family and friends …"

And so she did.

She Made a Difference

Gail Rosen, Storyteller

"Do you tell stories of the Holocaust?"

Hilda had been standing in front of me, with her back to me, talking to another woman, but she had heard me say, "I am a storyteller." We had just heard Hilda tell the story of her life in Germany from 1933 to 1945. We were at a *Yom HaShoah* (Holocaust memorial) event at the home of a friend.

"Do you tell stories of the Holocaust?"

"No," I said. "I don't feel entitled to tell them. They're not my stories. But they should be told. They need to be told, and I am grateful to have heard your story. I hope you continue to tell it for a long time, and I wonder who will tell it when you no longer tell it." Hilda looked me squarely in the eye and smiled without hesitation. "You tell it," she said.

In our conversations that followed, Hilda was open and generous in her willingness to enter into her most painful memories. The interviews covered life before the Nazis came to power through to her life with her beloved husband, children, and grandchildren. Hilda was gracious in her explanations, sharing her faith and her philosophy, welcoming me into her home and her synagogue.

I now tell Hilda's story in schools, synagogues, churches and other gatherings in the United States, in Germany, in Israel, and more recently in Poland. This book is a way to continue to tell her story. It is edited from our interviews (here printed in italics) and from writings (printed here in plain text) discovered by her husband after her death. Tucked away in a drawer, he found yellowed, fragile notebooks from Hilda's time in the Displaced Persons camp in Austria and a few entries from shortly after she arrived in the United States. There were over one hundred fifty poems, prose pieces, and letters. Following the war Hilda rarely wrote poetry, except for a few pieces in English, celebrating family events. She did write occasional articles and stories as well as journal entries.

Both her writing and the interviews reflect her intellect and honesty, her faith and devotion to Judaism, as well as the history of her personal experience. What moves me most about Hilda's life was her ability to live her ideals while at the same time being able to hold the dichotomy between her experience and her faith. She worshipped a merciful God, and she had flashbacks of the concentration camps. She was willing to look at the actions of the perpetrators beside her own humanity.

Because I tell Hilda's story, I have met people and had experiences that would never have happened otherwise. I have seen the impact of her poetry and her stories, especially in Germany.

I am grateful beyond words to have met Hilda Stern Cohen and to carry her story.

May her memory be a blessing.

Elborg Forster, Translator

Our work, indeed our life, sometimes takes us to places where we never expected to go.

Here I am, a woman born and educated in Germany who married an American academic and went on to live a comfortable, middle-class life in the United States for nearly fifty years, became a mother and grandmother, and spent many years as a busy translator of academic texts. History, sociology, anthropology, biography – much of it has been highly interesting, challenging, and broadening. And then in 2000, my work took a new turn, one that called for linguistic resources and emotional responses I did not know I could muster. I began translating poetry, German poetry written by a woman who was also born and educated in Germany, but who was a Jew and therefore cast headlong into the horrors of the Holocaust.

Of course I knew about the Holocaust. I knew firsthand about the hateful anti-Semitic propaganda that pervaded Germany in the 1930s – the "printed filth of screeching pamphlets" Hilda called it. I knew about the figures, six million Jews and others exterminated. I had even walked through the crematoria at Buchenwald and seen photographs of mounds of corpses and of emaciated survivors. But I had always kept all of this at arm's length, as it were: It was too painful.

And now the very personal work of a dead poet who had lived to turn horror into art was in my hands. I was challenged to use my long training in the art of translation to turn this German poetry into English poetry. But I was frightened. While I had read a good bit of poetry, I had never written any myself and translated very little. Furthermore, even a cursory reading of Hilda Stern Cohen's poetry showed me that many of the images and the very words she used belong to a realm of language that is as extreme as the experiences that gave rise to it. I had never entered that realm, but felt called upon to do so, for I came to understand that these writings must be made accessible to non-German speakers as important human testimony to a disaster that must never again be allowed to happen.

And so I started this work, remembering the words of my mentor at the University: "As philologists, we must never be afraid of words." And, I added to myself, "we must try to make the translation as powerful and as beautiful as the original."

Before long, feeling the need to know more about the background of these poems, I was led to read other poets of the Holocaust, as well as books about the Holocaust in general and the Lodz ghetto in particular. I also needed to know about Jewish culture in Germany, specifically as it related to women. And since Hilda Stern Cohen was a deeply religious woman, I had to learn about the religious, even mystical traditions to which she was so deeply committed.

I also gathered up the courage to visit the Holocaust Museum in Washington DC – a shattering experience, especially for one who lived in that Germany, albeit as a young child.

My efforts to render this poetry have expanded my horizons in unexpected ways. May they also make a small contribution to the healing of wounds.

William Gilcher, Co-Editor

On the last day of February 2001, Werner Cohen first walked into my office at the Goethe-Institut in Washington and asked me to look at his wife's poetry and help him find a way to get it published in Germany. How could I know how the experience of working with Hilda's work and life story would influence my life! In my work life, like most people, I deal with day-to-day tasks. Rarely do I get the chance to see how my work really makes a difference. After the publication of Hilda's collected works in Germany in 2003, I had the wonderful opportunity to travel with Werner Cohen and Gail Rosen for a series of story-telling events in Germany – including in Nieder-Ohmen, the lovely small town northeast of Frankfurt where Hilda was born. There we had the privilege of not only offering Hilda's story to the adults in the community, but were also asked to do a performance at the local school. When I looked at the faces of the school kids in Nieder-Ohmen as they listened to the story, I could see and hear them begin to understand that the events they read about in their textbooks happened to real people in their own country, indeed in their own hometown. And watching too, as Werner Cohen saw these children moved by hearing his wife's story, made me feel like I do something that is real, that is tangible in people's lives. It was one of the high points of my adult life.

Hearing Hilda's story and learning about her faith have helped me to gain greater understanding into the teachings of my own faith. It has also led me to try to understand first-hand what happened in places like Nieder-Ohmen and Frankfurt and also in Lodz and Auschwitz when hateful, but extraordinarily organized and systematic criminals were allowed to gain power in what was supposed to be a civilized, modern country. Strangely enough, the encounter with Hilda has also inspired me to compose music.

Most personally, I have learned about the Jewish idea that God did not complete creation, but that we are God's partners - that it is our responsibility to continue the creation, to help shape the moral world. This has changed the way I see my relationships with family and friends, with colleagues, and strangers I meet. What we do, how we treat each other is important for that continuing creation, and I know that more deeply now because of my encounter with this deeply human and deeply spiritual poet. I hope that many more people will now have an opportunity to encounter Hilda's words and message.

The Fate of the Jews in Nieder-Ohmen

by Heinrich Reichel, Nieder-Ohmen's town historian and a classmate of Hilda's, who knew all the Jews in the village personally.

In 1930 the population of Nieder-Ohmen was between thirteen hundred and fourteen hundred people. In 1940 the last Jews in Nieder-Ohmen had to leave the village, and the National Socialists reported that "Nieder-Ohmen is 'Jew-free.'"

Of the 92 Jewish citizens who were either registered in Nieder-Ohmen on December 31, 1932, moved here, or were born here after that date:

> 5 died in Nieder-Ohmen, probably of natural causes;
> 6 died elsewhere in Germany, probably of natural causes;
> 49 emigrated to America, England, Palestine, Turkey or other places;
> 32 died at the Nazis' hands or were murdered.

Until 1933, the Jews of Nieder-Ohmen thought of themselves as Germans of the Jewish faith. They were citizens of the village like everybody else and made up 6.4% of the total population. Nineteen Jews owned houses.

Jews and Christians had neighborly and business relations with each other. There were friendly relationships among the families. Almost all the Jews had businesses. There was no differentiation in the schools other than for religious instruction. After the Nazis came to power, many non-Jews continued to frequent Jewish businesses although it was forbidden. Many did this in secret and endangered themselves thereby. I know for instance in 1936 that craftsmen were required to post a sign in the window that said: "Jews Not Welcome Here." A cobbler had put the sign up in his shop in a spot that was relatively hard to see. Nazi officials came by and made him appear twice in one week in front of the local party leadership. A miller put the same sign up, also in a hard-to-see spot, but told his Jewish client that he would put his flour in the garden where it could be picked up in the evening.

Despite the fact that Nieder-Ohmen continued to have many non-Jewish citizens who resisted the anti-Semitic tide, the voters of Nieder-Ohmen, like those throughout the rural areas of Upper Hesse, favored the National Socialists to a degree that was considerably higher than the average in Germany. In the national parliamentary elections of November 1932, 65.2 per cent of those eligible to vote cast their ballots for the Nazis. This compares with 55.3 per cent in Upper Hesse and 33.1 per cent in Germany as a whole.

I hope that mankind here in Germany and in the community of Nieder-Ohmen have learned from the evil times of the Nazis (1933-1945) and will never again allow such a persecution and destruction of people and property, no matter what their religion or race might be.

The following text is now displayed on a plaque on the Town Hall:

As is amply documented, Jews have lived in Nieder-Ohmen since time immemorial. The Jewish Community numbered 70-80 members in the time before their persecution under the Third Reich. During the bestial regime of the Nazis, Jews were humiliated, disenfranchised and persecuted. Their fate must not be forgotten.

The Citizens of Nieder-Ohmen

Chronology

January 1, 1924   Hilde (later changed to Hilda in America) born in the village of Nieder-Ohmen, Hesse, Germany to Hedwig Stern, née Roth and Meier Stern, a farmer and trader in livestock.

1935   Because she is Jewish, Hilda is forced to leave the village school at age 11. She is sent to Frankfurt/Main to live with relatives and attends the Samson Raphael Hirsch School for a year.

1937-1938   Hilda attends the *Israelitische Lehrerbildungsanstalt* (ILBA), a Jewish Teacher-Training Institution in Würzburg.

November 9, 1938   After the *Kristallnacht* pogrom, ILBA is closed. Hilda's father is sent for four weeks to the Buchenwald Concentration Camp near Weimar in Thuringia.
The Stern family is required to sell their house, and the proceeds are seized. Hilda's father tries unsuccessfully to obtain visas to emigrate to the United States, where the family has relatives. The Stern family lives for a time in Frankfurt/Main.
After schools are closed, Hilda is assigned to forced labor. Her father is assigned to street construction.

February 1941   Hilda's sister Karola (later changed to Carol) is sent to Berlin as a forced laborer before being sent to Auschwitz in 1943.

October 21, 1941   Hilda and her parents are arrested in Frankfurt/Main by the Gestapo and deported by train to the "Litzmannstadt Ghetto" in Lodz, Poland as part of a transport of 1,186 Jews, including Hilda, her parents and maternal grandparents, and her friend Horst Appel.

Following their arrival, the Frankfurt Jews are housed initially in a school building at Hohensteiner Strasse (Zgierska) 70. Because of the impossibly crowded conditions, half of the group is moved to a building in an adjoining street, Storchengasse (Masarska) 22.

May 1942   Hilda, her parents, Horst Appel, and two others take up residence in the kitchen of a small apartment (housing more than twenty people) in an overcrowded building at Fischstrasse (Rybna) 14A. More than 320 people lived in this building during the period of the ghetto. The rolls list them with the following professions: artist painter, baker, bank employee, barber, bookkeeper, brush maker, building superintendant, cabinetmaker, capmaker, civil servant, cutter, darner, dealer, editor, engineer, farmer, fireman, fitter, glove-maker, hand-sewer, housewife, knitter, laborer, manufacturer, merchant, midwife, nurse, office clerk, office worker, packer, painter, paperhanger, plumber, porcelain painter, quilter, rabbi, schoolchild, seamstress, seminary student, storekeeper, sugarmaker, tailor, tanner, thread-twister, trainer, washerwoman, weaver.

June 9, 1942   Horst Appel dies at 23 of tuberculosis.

July 1942   Hilda's maternal grandparents, Jakob Roth and Sara Roth, née Kappenberg, die of starvation, aged 72 and 64.

March 1944   Hilda's mother, Hedwig Stern, née Roth, and her father, Meier Stern, die of illness and starvation, aged 41 and 52.

August 1944   Hilda is part of a last transport to leave for Auschwitz as the Nazis liquidate the Lodz ghetto.
On arrival in Auschwitz-Birkenau she is reunited with her sister Carol and is tattooed on her arm with the number 26011, a number that she could never recall from memory.

Early 1945   Evacuated from Auschwitz before the arrival of advancing Russian troops in an ordeal known as the "Death March."

May 3, 1945   Hilda and Carol are liberated in the woods outside the Malchow Concentration Camp near Berlin.

June 1945   The sisters travel on foot and by primitive transportation to Dobšina, a village in the Tatra Mountains of Slovakia.

Summer 1945   Arrival in Kammer-Schörfling, Austria, where they find various accommodations. Later, they find lodgings in the Hotel Mucha located at Schiffslände 17 on the Traunsee (lake) in nearby Gmunden. The hotel had been requisitioned for a military hospital, then for a "Displaced Persons Camp." During her time in Austria, Hilda writes down many compositions in such notebooks as she was able to find. The works include some prose pieces and many poems originally composed earlier in the war as well as new work describing and reacting to life as a displaced person.

July 29, 1946   The two sisters arrive in New York aboard the World War II liberty ship *Marine Marlin* after an eleven-day crossing from Bremerhaven, Germany.

September 5, 1948   Baltimore, Maryland: Hilda marries Werner V. Cohen, originally from Essen, Germany.

1952-1956   Three daughters, Hedy, Deborah, and Michele are born.

August 5, 1997   After a full, vibrant life as a Jewish teacher, mother, wife, and grandmother, Hilda dies in Baltimore, Maryland.
Shortly thereafter Werner V. Cohen discovers the notebooks with his wife's unpublished poetry and other compositions.

Fall 2003   Hilda's collected works are published in Germany.

Acknowledgements

The editors extend special thanks to the following persons for their encouragement and support over the long process of preparing this work:

Alan Adelson, *Jewish Heritage*, New York, for his careful reading and comments about the manuscript and for much useful advice about publishing;

Silke Berg, Frankfurt/Main, for use of the enhanced images created for the original German edition of Hilda's collected works;

Sascha Feuchert and **Erwin Leibfried**, of the *Research Center for Holocaust Literature* at the Justus-Liebig University, Giessen, for their immediate and enthusiastic interest in publishing Hilda's writing in German and for use of an image of Auschwitz-Birkenau in this volume;

Elborg Forster, for her extraordinary devotion to the task of translating into English all of Hilda Stern Cohen's poems – a selection of which are in this volume – as well as extensive pieces of prose. These tasks took her the better part of a year to complete;

Niv Goldberg, **Yad Vashem**, Jerusalem, for information about Izrael Lejzerowicz and permission to reproduce a drawing by the artist;

Merrill Leffler, *Dryad Press*, Takoma Park, Maryland, for his longstanding interest and useful advice about poetry and publishing;

Marianne Phelps, for her close reading of the manuscript and her many useful suggestions;

Heinrich Reichel, Nieder-Ohmen, for information about the history of Nieder-Ohmen and the photograph of the Stern home;

Carol Stern Steinhardt, Hilda's sister, for sharing information about the family and insights into her own experience during the Holocaust;

Rosemary Warschawski, for her editorial and design contributions as well as for her many thoughtful insights and encouragement over the years.

Continued from page 6

Layout and design: Anna-Maria Furlong, AMF Graphics, Texas

Printing: Edwards Brothers, Ann Arbor, Michigan

Two hundred copies of this first edition of *Words that Burn Within Me* have been numbered and signed by Werner V. Cohen